Docker for Serverless Applications

Containerize and orchestrate functions
using OpenFaas, OpenWhisk, and Fn

Chanwit Kaewkasi

BIRMINGHAM - MUMBAI

Docker for Serverless Applications

Commissioning Editor: Gebin George
Acquisition Editor: Rahul Nair
Content Development Editor: Nithin Varghese
Technical Editor: Vishal K. Mewada
Copy Editor: Safis Editing
Project Coordinator: Virginia Dias
Proofreader: Safis Editing
Indexer: Aishwarya Gangawane
Graphics: Tom Scaria
Production Coordinator: Nilesh Mohite

First published: April 2018

Production reference: 1180418

Published by Packt Publishing Ltd.
Livery Place
35 Livery Street
Birmingham
B3 2PB, UK.

ISBN 978-1-78883-526-8

www.packtpub.com

mapt.io

Mapt is an online digital library that gives you full access to over 5,000 books and videos, as well as industry leading tools to help you plan your personal development and advance your career. For more information, please visit our website.

Why subscribe?

- Spend less time learning and more time coding with practical eBooks and Videos from over 4,000 industry professionals

- Improve your learning with Skill Plans built especially for you

- Get a free eBook or video every month

- Mapt is fully searchable

- Copy and paste, print, and bookmark content

PacktPub.com

Did you know that Packt offers eBook versions of every book published, with PDF and ePub files available? You can upgrade to the eBook version at www.PacktPub.com and as a print book customer, you are entitled to a discount on the eBook copy. Get in touch with us at service@packtpub.com for more details.

At www.PacktPub.com, you can also read a collection of free technical articles, sign up for a range of free newsletters, and receive exclusive discounts and offers on Packt books and eBooks.

Contributors

About the author

Chanwit Kaewkasi is an assistant professor at the School of Computer Engineering, Suranaree University of Technology, Thailand. He started contributing code to the Docker Swarm project in its early day around 0.1. Later in 2016, he led the Swarm2K project together with contributors around the world to form the largest Docker Swarm cluster. Beside teaching and doing research in the field of software engineering, he provides consulting to several companies to help them adopt Docker, microservices, and FaaS technologies.

He currently serves the Docker community as a Docker Captain.

> *I would like to thank my wife, Pitchaya, for her endless support and encouragement. I also would like to thank my workplace, Suranaree University of Technology, to allow me to write this book as an academic work. My special thanks go to the editor team at Packt for their hard work, and to my reviewers for their invaluable comments.*
>
> *This book is dedicated to my parents, and all of my teachers.*

About the reviewer

Fabrizio Soppelsa works as a software engineer for Samsung, in the Next Platform and Containerization team. He spends most of his time integrating cloud components and making them perform faster. He's also an active Docker and Kubernetes contributor, and a Docker community leader.
He has published *Native Docker clustering with Swarm* for Packt.

In his spare time, he enjoys spending time with Anna, playing Go, traveling and taking care of his Russian canary Rambo.

Packt is searching for authors like you

If you're interested in becoming an author for Packt, please visit `authors.packtpub.com` and apply today. We have worked with thousands of developers and tech professionals, just like you, to help them share their insight with the global tech community. You can make a general application, apply for a specific hot topic that we are recruiting an author for, or submit your own idea.

Table of Contents

Preface

The container technology is very mature today. Docker, the software package that helps popularizing containers, is now being used by hundreds of thousands of developers as their day-to-day DevOps tool. I would say that Docker, the container engine, has now become a boring piece of software. For an infrastructure-level software package, boring means high quality and stability. I use it every day and I know you all use it as a part of your tool chain too. But we no longer feel excited when a new version of Docker is released. Just like what we feel to the releases of Linux kernels. With this feeling, the golden age of container has just recently passed, in my opinion.

The rise of Docker was in 2013. Its Renaissance was during 2014 - 2016. Many orchestration engine races between Docker Swarm and Kubernetes were at their peaks in 2016. One of them, the Swarm2K project, was my once-in-a-lifetime event. Docker later had an announcement to also support Kubernetes in 2017. The race ended there.

A couple of days ago, in March 2018, just before publishing this book, its founder, Solomon Hykes, left Docker Inc. Docker, the company, has been slowly and strongly moving from the startup world towards the enterprise business. What does this mean to us? Enterprise means stability, but startup means adventure. Let's move onto the new adventure, the post container—*the serverless era*.

What we will be talking about in this book is serverless. It is the natural evolution next to containers and microservices, in the different ways. First, a Docker container becomes a deployment unit for a function, a primitive unit-of-work in *the* Function-as-a-Service or FaaS architecture. Second, the microservices architecture has been gradually evolving to the FaaS architecture. FaaS could actually be anywhere on-premises or in the cloud. When the whole FaaS stack is managed by cloud providers, it becomes completely serverless.

But there will be something in between. Something is called *the hybrid serverless FaaS architecture*. This kind of architecture is the main idea I would like the readers to find out and enjoy in this book. It is the point where we could balance between costs, managing the servers by ourselves, and the degree of control we should have for our servers.

This book covers all three major FaaS platforms for Docker in detail, *OpenFaas*, *OpenWhisk* and *the Fn Project*. All of these projects are in their early stages and actively become more and more mature. So it is a great opportunity for the readers and me to learn and ride this new wave together. Let's do it.

Who this book is for

If you are a developer, a Docker engineer, a DevOps engineer, or any stakeholder interested in learning the use of Docker on serverless environments, then this book is for you.

If you are an undergrad or graduate student, this book is also for you to strengthen your knowledge in the area of *serverless and cloud computing*.

What this book covers

Chapter 1, *Serverless and Docker*, introduces serverless and Docker. We will find the relationship between them in this chapter. We will also learn the common architecture crystallized from studying architectures of several FaaS platforms. By the end of this chapter, we will learn how to say hello world using all three FaaS platforms, OpenFaaS, The Fn Project, and OpenWhisk.

Chapter 2, *Docker and Swarm Clusters*, reviews the container technology, namespaces and cgroups. Then, we will follow this by introducing Docker, how to install it, how to use its basic commands, and understand its workflow for build, ship, and run. Continuing further, we will then move to review its built-in orchestration engine, Docker Swarm. We will learn how to set up a cluster and see how Docker Swarm works internally. We will then learn how to set up a Docker network, attach it to containers, and how to scale services in Docker Swarm.

Chapter 3, *Serverless Frameworks*, discusses serverless frameworks, including platforms such as AWS Lambda, Google Cloud Functions, Azure Functions, and IBM Cloud Functions. We will end this chapter with a FaaS platform-independent framework, the serverless framework.

Chapter 4, *OpenFaaS on Docker*, explains how to use OpenFaaS. We will explore its architecture and components. Then we will learn how to prepare, build, and deploy functions with its provided tools and templates, how to prepare its cluster on top of Swarm, how to use its user interface, and how OpenFaaS leverages Docker multi-stage build. And we will also discuss how to use Prometheus to monitor the FaaS platform.

Chapter 5, *The Fn Project*, explores another FaaS platform. Similar to Chapter 4, *OpenFaaS on Docker*, we will start with its architecture and components, then go through a set of CLI commands to build, package, and deploy functions to Fn. Later in this chapter, we will learn how to monitor the platform using its built-in UI. Also, we will use a familiar tool to help analyze its logs.

Chapter 6, *OpenWhisk on Docker*, discusses OpenWhisk, the third and final FaaS platform for this book. We will walk through its concept and architecture.

Chapter 7, *Operating FaaS Clusters*, speaks about several techniques of preparing and operating production-grade FaaS clusters using Docker Swarm. We will discuss how to replace the whole layer of networking with another easy-to-use container networking plugin. We will also show how to implement the new routing mesh mechanism to avoid bugs from the current ingress implementation. Also, we will discuss some advanced topics such as *distributed tracing* and how to implement it. We will even cover the concept of cost reduction with spot instances and how to implement Swarm on this dynamic infrastructure.

Chapter 8, *Putting Them All Together*, explains how to implement a heterogeneous FaaS system combining all three FaaS platforms running seamlessly together on a robust product-grade Swarm cluster. We will show a mobile-based bank transfer use case, also with a legacy wrapper, a mobile backend WebHook, and stream data processing with FaaS. A bonus here is we also add a blockchain to the use case to show their interoperation.

Chapter 9, *The Future of Serverless,* concludes this book with advanced concepts and research prototype implementations that go beyond the current serverless and FaaS technologies.

To get the most out of this book

The reader should know the basics of Linux and Docker commands. Although this is optional, it would be a big plus if the reader has a basic understanding of network protocols and has some familiarity to the cloud computing concepts.

Although it is possible to use a MacBook or PC with Windows OS to run examples in this book, it is highly recommended for the reader to use Ubuntu Linux 16.04 and above. The reader with Mac book or Windows could run examples via Linux on a virtual machine, or a cloud instance.

Download the example code files

You can download the example code files for this book from your account at www.packtpub.com. If you purchased this book elsewhere, you can visit www.packtpub.com/support and register to have the files emailed directly to you.

You can download the code files by following these steps:

1. Log in or register at www.packtpub.com.
2. Select the **SUPPORT** tab.
3. Click on **Code Downloads & Errata**.
4. Enter the name of the book in the **Search** box and follow the onscreen instructions.

Once the file is downloaded, please make sure that you unzip or extract the folder using the latest version of:

- WinRAR/7-Zip for Windows
- Zipeg/iZip/UnRarX for Mac
- 7-Zip/PeaZip for Linux

The code bundle for the book is also hosted on GitHub at https://github.com/PacktPublishing/Docker-for-Serverless-Applications. In case there's an update to the code, it will be updated on the existing GitHub repository.

We also have other code bundles from our rich catalog of books and videos available at https://github.com/PacktPublishing/. Check them out!

Conventions used

There are a number of text conventions used throughout this book.

code in text: Indicates code words in text, database table names, folder names, filenames, file extensions, pathnames, dummy URLs, user input, and Twitter handles. Here is an example: "We will try the echoit function to hello world with OpenFaaS."

A block of code is set as follows:

```
FROM ubuntu
RUN apt-get update && apt-get install -y nginx
EXPOSE 80
ENTRYPOINT ["nginx", "-g", "daemon off;"]
```

Any command-line input or output is written as follows:

```
$ curl -sSL https://get.docker.com | sudo sh
$ docker swarm init --advertise-addr=eth0
```

Bold: Indicates a new term, an important word, or words that you see onscreen. For example, words in menus or dialog boxes appear in the text like this. Here is an example: "The following screenshot shows the browser running **OpenFaaS Portal**."

Warnings or important notes appear like this.

Tips and tricks appear like this.

Get in touch

Feedback from our readers is always welcome.

General feedback: Email `feedback@packtpub.com` and mention the book title in the subject of your message. If you have questions about any aspect of this book, please email us at `questions@packtpub.com`.

Errata: Although we have taken every care to ensure the accuracy of our content, mistakes do happen. If you have found a mistake in this book, we would be grateful if you would report this to us. Please visit `www.packtpub.com/submit-errata`, selecting your book, clicking on the Errata Submission Form link, and entering the details.

Piracy: If you come across any illegal copies of our works in any form on the Internet, we would be grateful if you would provide us with the location address or website name. Please contact us at `copyright@packtpub.com` with a link to the material.

If you are interested in becoming an author: If there is a topic that you have expertise in and you are interested in either writing or contributing to a book, please visit `authors.packtpub.com`.

Reviews

Please leave a review. Once you have read and used this book, why not leave a review on the site that you purchased it from? Potential readers can then see and use your unbiased opinion to make purchase decisions, we at Packt can understand what you think about our products, and our authors can see your feedback on their book. Thank you!

For more information about Packt, please visit `packtpub.com`.

1
Serverless and Docker

When talking about containers, most of us already know how to pack an application into a container as a deployment unit. Docker allows us to deploy applications in its *de facto* standard format to virtually everywhere, ranging from our laptop, a QA cluster, a customer site, or a public cloud, as shown in the following diagram:

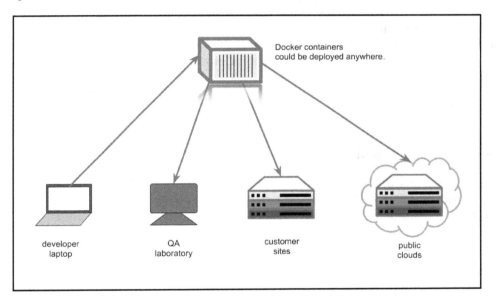

Figure 1.1: Deploying a Docker container to various infrastructures and platforms

Running Docker containers on public clouds is considered normal these days. We have already gained benefits such as starting cloud instances on demand with pay-as-you-go billing. Without the need to wait for hardware purchase, we can also move faster using an Agile method with a continuous delivery pipeline to optimize our resources.

According to a Docker report, the **total cost of ownership** (**TCO**) of one of their customers was cut by 66% when using Docker to migrate existing applications to the cloud. Not only can the TCO be dramatically reduced, the companies using Docker can also accelerate the time to market from months to days. This is a huge win.

Deploying containers to cloud infrastructures, such as AWS, Google Cloud, or Microsoft Azure, already makes things simpler. Cloud infrastructures eliminate the need for organizations to buy their own hardware and to have a dedicated team for maintaining it.

However, organizations still require the role, such as that of the architect, to take care of site reliability and scalability even when they use the public cloud infrastructure. Some of these people are known as **SREs**, the **site reliability engineers**.

In addition, organizations also need to take care of system-level packages and dependencies. They need to perform patching for application security and the OS kernel on their own because the software stack will be constantly changing. In many scenarios, the team in these organizations must scale the size of their clusters to unexpectedly serve requests when loads are peaking. Also, the engineers need to do their best to scale the clusters down, when possible, so as to reduce the cloud costs as it is a pay-as-you-go model.

Developers and engineering teams always work hard to deliver great user experience and site availability. While doing that, over provisioning on-demand instances or under utilizing them, can be costly. According to an AWS white paper, `https://d0.awsstatic.com/whitepapers/optimizing-enterprise-economics-serverless-architectures.pdf`, the amount of underutilized instances is as much as 85% of the provisioned machines.

Serverless computing platforms, such as AWS Lambda, Google Cloud Functions, Azure Functions, and IBM Cloud Functions, are designed to address these overprovisioning and underutilization problems.

The following topics will be covered in this chapter:

- Serverless
- The common architecture of a serverless FaaS
- Serverless/FaaS use cases
- Hello world, the FaaS/Docker way

What is serverless?

Try to imagine that we live in a world fully driven by software with a kind of intelligence.

It would be a world where we could develop software without doing anything. Just say what kind of software we would like to run, and minutes later, it would be there somewhere on the internet serving many users. And we would only pay for the number of requests made by our users. Well, that kind of world is too unreal.

Now, let's be more realistic and think of the world where we still need to develop software by ourselves. At least for now, we do not need to take care of any server provisioning and management. This is actually, at least, the best world for developers, where we can deploy our applications to reach millions of users without taking care of any server, or even not needing to know where these servers are. The only thing we actually want is to create an application that addresses the needs of the business at scale, at an affordable price. The serverless platforms have been created to address these problems.

As a response to developers and fast-growing businesses, serverless platforms seem to be a very huge win. But what exactly are they?

The relationship between serverless and FaaS

The following diagram illustrates the position of event-driven programming, FaaS, and serverless FaaS, where serverless FaaS is the intersection area between FaaS and serverless:

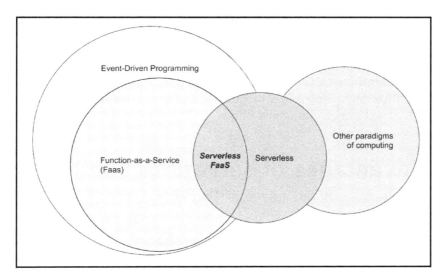

Figure 1.2: A Venn diagram illustrating the relationship between serverless and FaaS

Serverless is a paradigm shift that enables developers to not worry about server provisioning and operations. Billing would be pay-per-request. Also, many useful services are there on the public cloud for us to choose, connecting them together and use them to solve the business problems to get the job done.

Applications in the serverless architecture typically use third-party services to do other jobs such as authentication, database systems, or file storage. It is not necessary for serverless applications to use these third-party services, but architecting the application this way takes full advantage of the cloud-based serverless platforms. The frontend applications in this kind of architecture are usually a thick, fat, and powerful frontend, such as single-page applications or mobile applications.

The execution engine for this serverless computing shift is a **Function as a Service** or **FaaS** platform. A FaaS platform is a computing engine, that allows us to write a simple, self-contained, single-purpose function to process or compute a task. A compute unit of a FaaS platform is a function that is recommended to be stateless. This stateless property makes functions fully manageable and scalable by the platform.

A FaaS platform does not necessarily run on a serverless environment, such as AWS Lambda, but there are many FaaS implementations, such as OpenFaaS, the Fn Project, and OpenWhisk, that allow us to deploy and run FaaS on our own hardware. If a FaaS platform runs in the serverless environment, it would be called **serverless FaaS**. For example, we have OpenWhisk running locally, so it is our FaaS platform. But when it is running on IBM Cloud as IBM Cloud Functions, it is a serverless FaaS.

Every FaaS platform has been designed to use the event-driven programming model, to be able to connect efficiently to other services on the public cloud. With the asynchronous event model and the stateless property of functions, this environment makes serverless FaaS an ideal model for next-generation computing.

The disadvantages of serverless FaaS

But what are the drawbacks of this approach? They are as follows:

- We basically do not own the servers. The serverless model is not suitable when we need fine-grained control over our infrastructure.

- Serverless FaaS has a lot of limitations, notably the time limits of function execution, and memory limits for each function instance. It also introduces a fixed and specific way to develop applications. Maybe it is a bit hard to migrate the existing systems directly to FaaS.
- It is impossible to fully use serverless platforms with private or hybrid infrastructure, if we are not allowed to migrate all workload out of the organization. One of the real benefits of serverless architectures is the existence of convenient public services on the cloud.

Docker to the rescue

This book discusses the balance between FaaS on our own infrastructure and serverless FaaS. We try to simplify and unify the deployment model of FaaS by choosing three major FaaS platforms that allow us to deploy Docker containers as functions, which we discuss in this book.

With Docker containers as deployment units (functions), Docker as a development tool, and Docker as the orchestration engine and networking layer, we can develop serverless applications and deploy them on our available hardware, on our own private cloud infrastructure, or a hybrid cloud that mixes our hardware together with the public cloud's hardware.

One of the most important points is that it is easy enough to take care of this kind of infrastructure using a small team of developers with Docker skills.

Looking back the previous *Figure 1.2*. If you're getting the clue after reading this chapter up to here, let's guess a bit that what would be the contents to be discussed in this book. Where should we be in this diagram? The answer is at the end of this chapter.

Common architecture of a serverless FaaS

Before getting into other technical chapters, the common architecture of at least six serverless FaaS platforms surveyed and studied during the writing of this book is presented in the following diagram. It is a distilled overview of the existing FaaS platforms and a recommended architecture, if you want to create a new one:

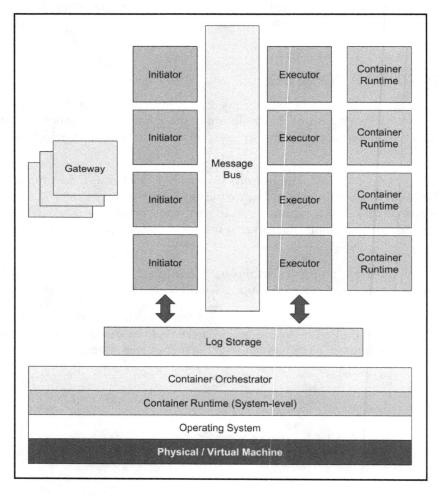

Figure 1.3: A block diagram describing the common architecture for FaaS platforms

System layers

A description of the architecture from bottom to top is as follows:

- We have some physical or virtual machines. These machines could be on a public or private cloud. Some of them may be a physical box running inside a firewall or an organization. They may be mixed together as a hybrid infrastructure.
- The next layer is the **Operating System** and, of course, the kernels. We need an OS with a modern kernel that supports container isolation, such as Linux, or that is at least compatible with runC. Windows or Windows Server 2016 has its own Hyper-V based isolation that is compatible with Docker.
- The next layer in the architecture is the **Container Runtime (System-Level)**. We emphasize that it is the system-level container runtime as it is not for running FaaS functions directly. This layer is responsible for provisioning the cluster.
- Next is the optional container orchestration engine, or **Container Orchestrator**, layer. This layer is Docker Swarm or Kubernetes. We use Docker Swarm in this book, but you may find that some FaaS platforms presented in this book do not use any kind of orchestration. Basically, just Docker alone with container networking is enough for a FaaS platform to get up and running effectively.

FaaS layers

Now, we will discuss the actual FaaS layers. We will go from left to right:

- The frontier component of the whole architecture is the FaaS **Gateway**. The gateway in some implementations is optional, but in many implementations, this component helps serve HTTPS and cache some static content, such as UI parts, of the platform. Gateway instances help for making better throughput. It is usually a stateless HTTP-based reverse proxy. So this component is easy to scale-out.
- The **Initiator** is one of the most important components of FaaS. An initiator is responsible for imitating the real invocation request to the rest of the platform. In OpenWhisk, this component is called the **controller,** for example. In Fn, the part inside its Fn server acts as the **Initiator**.
- The **Message Bus** is the message backbone of a FaaS platform. Some architectures that do not have this component will have a difficulty to properly implement asynchronous calls, or the retry pattern to make the platform robust. The message bus decouples initiators out of executors.

- The **Executor** is the component that does the real function invocation. It connects to its own container runtime (application-level) to start the real sequence of function execution. All results and logging will be written to the central log storage.
- **Log Storage** is the platform's single source of truth. It should be designed to store almost everything, ranging from the function activities to the error logs of each invocation.
- **Container Runtime** (application level) is a component responsible for starting the function container. We simply use Docker and its underlying engine as the runtime component in this book.

Serverless/FaaS use cases

Serverless/FaaS is a generic computing model. Therefore, it would be possible to implement virtually any kind of workloads using this programming paradigm. The use cases of serverless/FaaS could range from an API for normal web applications, a RESTful backend for mobile applications, a function for log or video processing, a backend for WebHook-based systems, to a stream data processing program:

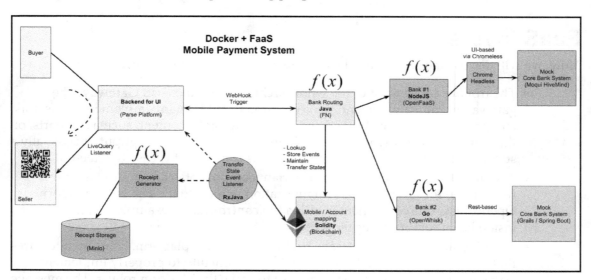

Figure 1.4: The block diagram of the demo project

In `Chapter 8`, *Putting Them all Together*, we will discuss a system, as shown in the previous diagram, with the following use cases:

- APIs for a WebHook-based system: In the previous diagram, you may have spotted the **Backend for UI**. This system allows us to define a WebHook and it will be implemented as a FaaS function using one of the frameworks discussed in a later chapter.
- APIs to wrap around a legacy system: In the upper right-hand corner of the previous diagram, we will find a set of functions connecting to a **Chrome Headless** (a fully-functional running Google Chrome instance). The function there wraps around a set of commands to instruct Google Chrome to work on a legacy system for us.
- APIs as abstractions for other services: In the lower right-hand corner there are two simple blocks. The first one is a function running on a FaaS platform connecting to the second one, **Mock Core Bank System**, which is a more complex REST API. This part of the system demonstrates how a FaaS function could be used as an abstraction to simplify the interface of a complex system.
- Stream data processing: We will also implement a data processing agent, an event listener, which listens to an event source—you may find the *Ethereum logo* there with a circle that connects from the left. This agent will listen to the data stream from the source and then call a function running on a FaaS platform.

Hello world, the FaaS/Docker way

This book covers all three major frameworks of FaaS on Docker. So it would not be fair, if I were the one to choose a specific framework for the *hello world* program in this first chapter. I will let you choose one from your very own preference.

The following is the common setup on a Linux machine. For Mac or Windows users, please skip this step and download Docker for Mac, or Docker for Windows:

```
$ curl -sSL https://get.docker.com | sudo sh
```

If you choose to go with OpenFaaS in this chapter, you can simplify this setup process by using *Play with Docker* (`https://labs.play-with-docker.com/`), which automatically installs OpenFaaS on a single-node Docker Swarm.

When we get Docker installed, just initialize Swarm to make our single-node cluster ready to run:

```
$ docker swarm init --advertise-addr=eth0
```

If the previous command failed, try changing the network interface name to match yours. But if it still fails, just put one of the machine's IP addresses there.

If everything is set up successfully, let's start the series of hello world programs on various FaaS platforms.

Hello OpenFaas

We will try the `echoit` function to `hello world` with OpenFaaS. First, clone the project from `https://github.com/openfaas/faas` with one level of depth to just make the clone process quicker:

```
$ git clone --depth=1 https://github.com/openfaas/faas
```

Then, change the directory into `faas`, and simply deploy the OpenFaaS default stack, using the following command:

```
$ cd faas
$ docker stack deploy -c docker-compose.yml func
```

Wait until the stack is going up. Then, we do `hello world` with the `curl` command:

```
$ curl -d "hello world." -v http://localhost:8080/function/func_echoit
* Trying 127.0.0.1...
* Connected to localhost (127.0.0.1) port 8080 (#0)
> POST /function/func_echoit HTTP/1.1
> Host: localhost:8080
> User-Agent: curl/7.47.0
> Accept: */*
> Content-Length: 12
> Content-Type: application/x-www-form-urlencoded
>
* upload completely sent off: 12 out of 12 bytes
< HTTP/1.1 200 OK
< Content-Length: 12
< Content-Type: application/x-www-form-urlencoded
< Date: Fri, 23 Mar 2018 16:37:30 GMT
< X-Call-Id: 866c9294-e243-417c-827c-fe0683c652cd
< X-Duration-Seconds: 0.000886
< X-Start-Time: 1521823050543598099
```

```
<
* Connection #0 to host localhost left intact
hello world.
```

After playing around it, we could also use `docker stack rm` to remove all running services:

```
$ docker stack rm func
```

Hello OpenWhisk

Let's quickly move to OpenWhisk. To `hello world` with OpenWhisk, we also need a `docker-compose` binary. Please visit `https://github.com/docker/compose/releases` and follow instructions there to install it.

With OpenWhisk, the whole stack would be a bit longer to get up and running than with OpenFaaS. But the overall command will be simpler as the `hello world` is already built in.

First, clone the OpenWhisk development tool from its GitHub repository:

```
$ git clone --depth=1
https://github.com/apache/incubator-openwhisk-devtools devtools
```

Then change the directory into `devtools/docker-compose`, and manually do image pulling, using the following commands:

```
$ cd devtools/docker-compse
$ docker-compose pull
$ docker pull openwhisk/nodejs6action
```

After that, just call `make quick-start` to perform the setup:

```
$ make quick-start
```

Wait until the OpenWhisk cluster has started. This could take up to 10 minutes.

After that, run the following command, `make hello-world`, to register and invoke the `hello world` action:

```
$ make hello-world
creating the hello.js function ...
invoking the hello-world function ...
adding the function to whisk ...
ok: created action hello
invoking the function ...
```

```
invokation result: { "payload": "Hello, World!" }
{ "payload": "Hello, World!" }
deleting the function ...
ok: deleted action hello
```

Make sure that you're on a fast internet connection. The slowness associated with OpenWhisk pulling the invoke and controller often causes make quick-start to fail.

To clean up, just use the make destroy command to terminate the target:

```
$ make destroy
```

Say hello to the Fn project

This is another FaaS project covered by this book. We quickly do hello world by installing the Fn CLI. Then use it to start a local Fn server, create an app, and then create a route that links to a pre-built Go function under the app. After that, we will use the curl command to test the deployed hello world function.

Here's the standard command to install the Fn client:

```
$ curl -LSs https://raw.githubusercontent.com/fnproject/cli/master/install
| sudo sh
```

After that, we can use the fn command. Let's start an Fn server. Use --detach to make it run in the background:

```
$ fn start --detach
```

Well, if we see a container ID, it is good to go. Next, quickly create an Fn app and call it goapp:

```
$ fn apps create goapp
```

Then, we already have a pre-built image called chanwit/fn_ch1:0.0.2 on the Docker Hub. Just use it. We use the fn routes create command to link the new route to the image. The purpose of this step is to actually define a function:

```
$ fn routes create --image chanwit/fn_ch1:0.0.2 goapp /fn_ch1
/fn_ch1 created with chanwit/fn_ch1:0.0.2
```

OK, the route is ready. Now, we can use the `curl` command to just call our `hello world` program on Fn:

```
$ curl -v http://localhost:8080/r/goapp/fn_ch1
* Trying 127.0.0.1...
* Connected to localhost (127.0.0.1) port 8080 (#0)
> GET /r/goapp/fn_ch1 HTTP/1.1
> Host: localhost:8080
> User-Agent: curl/7.47.0
> Accept: */*
>
< HTTP/1.1 200 OK
< Content-Length: 26
< Content-Type: application/json; charset=utf-8
< Fn_call_id: 01C99YJXCE47WG200000000000
< Xxx-Fxlb-Wait: 383.180124ms
< Date: Fri, 23 Mar 2018 17:30:34 GMT
<
{"message":"Hello World"}
* Connection #0 to host localhost left intact
```

OK, it seems all things are working as well as expected for Fn. Let's remove the server after it has finished:

```
$ docker rm -f fnserver
```

Exercise

At the end of every chapter, there will be a set of questions to help us review the content of the current chapter. Let's try to answer each of them without going back to the chapter's contents:

1. What is the definition of serverless?
2. What is the definition of FaaS?
3. Describe the difference between FaaS and serverless?
4. What are the roles of Docker in the world of serverless applications?
5. What does the common architecture of FaaS look like?

6. Try to explain why we are in the shaded area in the following diagram:

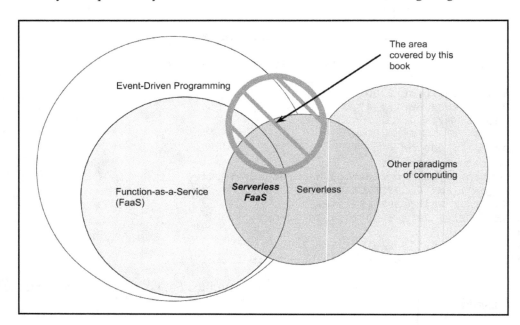

Figure 1.5: Scope of FaaS and serverless area covered by this book

Summary

This chapter has introduced serverless and Docker, the definition of serverless, and the definition of FaaS. We learned the benefits of serverless, when to use it, and when to avoid it. A serverless FaaS is a FaaS platform run by a vendor on a public cloud, while a FaaS may be required to run on a private, a hybrid, or an on-premises environment. This is where we can use Docker. Docker will help us build FaaS applications, and prepare container infrastructure to run container-based functions.

We previewed the demo project that will be built step by step in later chapters. We then quickly did `hello world` with all three leading FaaS platforms for Docker to demonstrate how easy it is to run FaaS platforms on our own Docker cluster.

In the next chapter, we will review the concepts of the container, and the technologies behind it. We will also introduce Docker and its workflow, then we will learn the concept of the Docker Swarm cluster and how to prepare it. And finally, we will discuss how Docker fits into the world of serverless.

Docker and Swarm Clusters 2

In this chapter, we will review container technology and introduce Docker and its orchestration engine, as well as Docker Swarm mode. We will then discuss why we need a Docker infrastructure to deploy and run serverless and FaaS applications. The topics covered in this chapter are as follows:

- Containers and Docker
- Setting up a Docker Swarm cluster
- Performing container networking with Docker
- Why Docker fits into the serverless and FaaS infrastructure

What is a container?

Before talking about Docker, it would be better to discuss the technology behind the software container.

Virtual machines are a common virtualization technology and have been widely adopted by cloud providers and enterprise companies. Actually, a software container (or container for short) is also a kind of virtualization technology, but there is something different about them. The key difference is that every container shares the same kernel on the host machine, while each virtual machine has its own kernel. Basically, a container uses virtualization techniques at the level of the operating system, not the *hypervisor*. The following diagram shows a comparison between container and VM stacks:

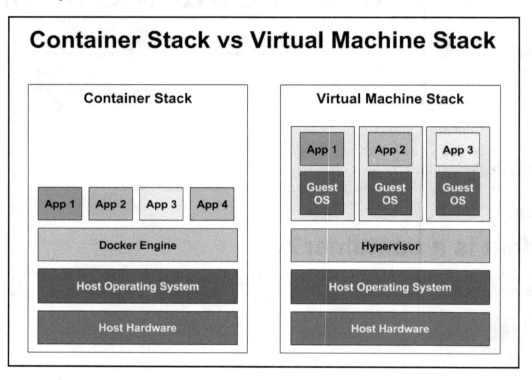

Figure 2.1: Containers versus virtual machines

Linux's container technology heavily relies on two important kernel capabilities, **namespace** and **cgroups**. Namespace puts a process into isolation so it has its own of set of global resources, such as PIDs and networks. Cgroups or control groups provide a mechanism for metering and limiting resources, such as CPU usage, memory, block I/O, and network bandwidth:

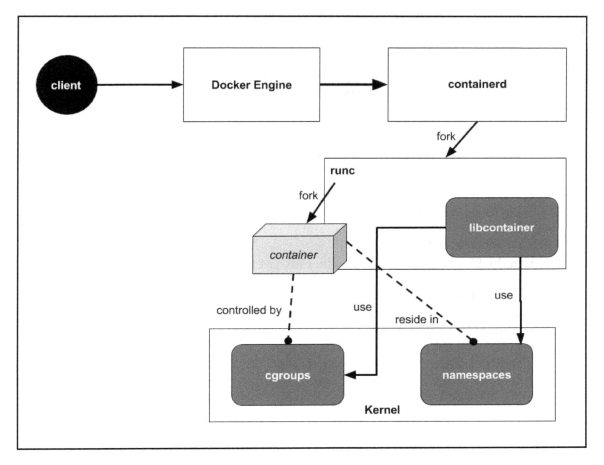

Figure 2.2: Linux capabilities—namespaces and cgroups used by a container

The core engine that uses the **namespaces** and **cgroups** capabilities of Linux is called **runC**. It is a tool for spawning and running containers in the **Open Container Initiative** (**OCI**) format. Docker plays a major role in drafting this spec, so the Docker container image is compatible with OCI specifications and therefore runnable by runC. The Docker Engine itself uses *runC* underneath to start each container.

What is Docker?

Containers in the past were quite difficult to manage and use. Docker is basically a set of technologies to help us prepare, manage, and execute containers. In the world of virtual machines, we need a hypervisor to take care of all VM instances. Similarly, in the world of containers, we use Docker as the *container engine* to take care of everything to do with containers.

Undeniably, Docker is the most popular container engine to date. When using Docker, we follow the three concepts build, ship, and run, recommended by Docker itself:

- The workflow of **Build-Ship-Run** is optimized by the philosophy of Docker. In the **Build** step, we are allowed to build and destroy container images rapidly. As developers, we can include the container building steps as a part of our development cycle.
- In the **Ship** step, we ship container images to places, from our development laptops to the QA servers and to the staging servers. We send the container images to be stored in the public hub or to our private registry hub inside our company. Ultimately, we send our container images to run in the production environment.
- In the **Run** step, Docker helps us prepare the production environment with Swarm clusters. We start containers from the container images. We may schedule containers to run at a specific part of the cluster with a certain set of constraints. We manage a container's life cycle using Docker commands:

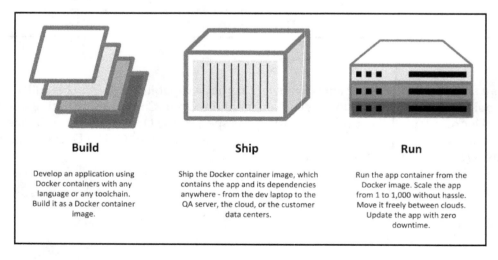

Build

Develop an application using Docker containers with any language or any toolchain. Build it as a Docker container image.

Ship

Ship the Docker container image, which contains the app and its dependencies anywhere - from the dev laptop to the QA server, the cloud, or the customer data centers.

Run

Run the app container from the Docker image. Scale the app from 1 to 1,000 without hassle. Move it freely between clouds. Update the app with zero downtime.

Figure 2.3: Build-ship-run

Installing Docker

Before we follow the build-ship-run steps, we need to install Docker on our machine. On Linux, we use the classic installation method, **Docker Community Edition** (**CE** or **Docker-CE**):

```
$ curl -sSL https://get.docker.com | sudo bash
```

Throughout the book, we will use a Debian or Ubuntu machine to demonstrate Docker. On a Debian/Ubuntu machine, we will get the most stable version of Docker (at the time of writing) via `apt-get` Docker back to version 17.06.2. If we already have a newer version of Docker, such as 17.12 or 18.03, it will be downgraded to 17.06.2:

```
$ sudo apt-get install docker-ce=17.06.2~ce-0~ubuntu
```

For macOS and Windows systems, we can download Docker from the Docker website:

- Docker for Mac: `https://www.docker.com/docker-mac`
- Docker for Windows: `https://www.docker.com/docker-windows`

To check the installed version of Docker, we can use the `docker version` command:

```
$ docker version

Client:
 Version: 17.06.2-ce
 API version: 1.30
 Go version: go1.8.3
 Git commit: cec0b72
 Built: Tue Sep 5 20:00:33 2017
 OS/Arch: linux/amd64

Server:
 Version: 17.06.2-ce
 API version: 1.30 (minimum version 1.12)
 Go version: go1.8.3
 Git commit: cec0b72
 Built: Tue Sep 5 19:59:26 2017
 OS/Arch: linux/amd64
 Experimental: true
```

The information printed out from the `docker version` is separated into two sections, client and server. The client section tells us information about the `docker` binary used to issue commands. The server section tells us the version of `dockerd`, the Docker Engine.

What we can see from the previous snippet is that both client and server are of version 17.06.2-ce, the second update of the stable 17.06 Community Edition. The server allows Docker client 1.12 as the minimum version to connect to. The *API version* tells us that `dockerd` implements remote API version 1.30.

If we expect to use the next stable version of Docker, we should go for the upcoming 17.06.3, 17.09.x, or 17.12.x versions.

Building a container image

We use Docker to prepare our software and its execution environment by packing them onto a file system. We call this step building a container image. OK, let's do this. We will build our own version of an NGINX server on Ubuntu, `my-nginx`, as a Docker image. Please note that the terms container image and Docker image will be used interchangeably throughout this book.

We create a directory called `my-nginx` and change to it:

```
$ mkdir my-nginx
$ cd my-nginx
```

Then, we create a file named Dockerfile with the following content:

```
FROM ubuntu
RUN apt-get update && apt-get install -y nginx
EXPOSE 80
ENTRYPOINT ["nginx", "-g", "daemon off;"]
```

We will explain the contents of Dockerfile line by line:

- First, it says that we want to use the image named `ubuntu` as our base image. This `ubuntu` image is stored on the Docker Hub, a central image registry server hosted by Docker Inc.
- Second, it says that we want to install NGINX and related packages using the `apt-get` command. The trick here is that `ubuntu` is a plain Ubuntu image without any package information, so we need to run `apt-get update` before installing packages.
- Third, we want this image to open port `80`, *inside the container*, for our NGINX server.
- Finally, when we start a container from this image, Docker will run the `nginx -g daemon off;` command inside the container for us.

We are now ready to build our first Docker image. Type the following command to start building an image. Please note that there is *dot* at the end of the command:

```
$ docker build -t my-nginx .
```

You will now see something similar to the following output with different hash numbers, so don't worry. Steps 2 to 4 will take a couple of minutes to finish, as it will download and install NGINX packages into the image filesystem. Just make sure that there are four steps and it ends with the message Successfully tagged my-nginx:latest:

```
Sending build context to Docker daemon 2.048kB
Step 1/4 : FROM ubuntu
 ---> ccc7a11d65b1
Step 2/4 : RUN apt-get update && apt-get install -y nginx
 ---> Running in 1f95e93426d3
. . .
Step 3/4 : EXPOSE 8080
 ---> Running in 4f84a2dc1b28
 ---> 8b89cae986b0
Removing intermediate container 4f84a2dc1b28
Step 4/4 : ENTRYPOINT nginx -g daemon off;
 ---> Running in d0701d02a092
 ---> 0a393c45ed34
Removing intermediate container d0701d02a092
Successfully built 0a393c45ed34
Successfully tagged my-nginx:latest
```

We now have a Docker image called my-nginx:latest locally on our machine. We can check that the image is really there using the docker image ls command (or docker images for the old-style, top-level command):

```
$ docker image ls
REPOSITORY   TAG      IMAGE ID      CREATED          SIZE
my-nginx     latest   0a393c45ed34  18 minutes ago   216MB
```

Basically, this is the *build* concept of Docker. Next, we continue with shipping images.

Shipping an image

We usually ship Docker images via a Docker registry. The public registry hosted by Docker Inc. is called **Docker Hub**. To ship a Docker image to a registry, we use the `docker push` command. When we start a container, its image will be automatically checked and downloaded to the host before running. The process of downloading can be explicitly done using the `docker pull` command. The following diagram illustrates the push/pull behavior among different environments and registries:

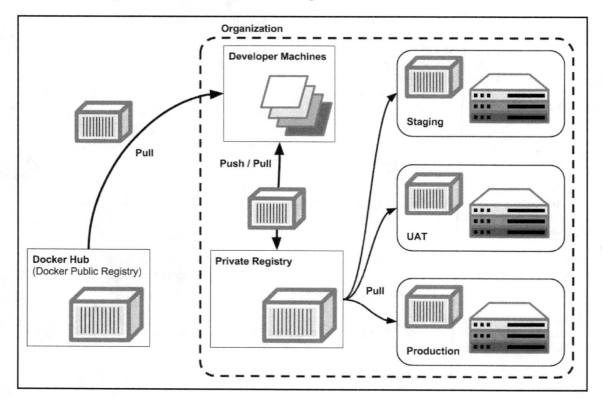

Figure 2.4: Push and pull image workflow

In the previous diagram, developers pull images from the Docker public registry (Docker Hub) then push and pull images from their own Docker private registry. In the development environment, each environment will be triggered by a mechanism to pull images there and run them.

To check that our Docker daemon is allowed to interact with a Docker registry insecurely over the non-encrypted HTTP, we do `docker info` then `grep` for the `Registries` keyword.

> Please note that the insecure Docker registry is not recommended for a production environment. You have been warned!

```
$ docker info | grep -A3 Registries
Insecure Registries:
 127.0.0.0/8
Live Restore Enabled: false
```

OK, seeing `127.0.0.0/8` means that we are allowed to do so. We will have a local Docker registry running at `127.0.0.1:5000`. Let's set it up.

To have a local Docker registry running, just run it from the Docker registry V2 image:

```
$ docker container run --name=registry -d -p 5000:5000 registry:2
6f7dc5ef89f070397b93895527ec2571f77e86b8d2beea2d8513fb30294e3d10
```

We should check if it is now up and running:

```
$ docker container ls --filter name=registry
CONTAINER ID  IMAGE       COMMAND            CREATED        STATUS
6f7dc5ef89f0  registry:2  "/entrypoint.sh /e.."  8 seconds ago  Up
```

The details of `container run` and other commands will be discussed again in the *Running a container* section.

Recall that we have built an image named `my-nginx`. We can check if it is still there; this time we use `--filter reference` to select only an image name ending with `nginx`:

```
$ docker image ls --filter reference=*nginx
REPOSITORY  TAG     IMAGE ID      CREATED       SIZE
my-nginx    latest  a773a4303694  1 days ago    216MB
nginx       latest  b8efb18f159b  2 months ago  107MB
```

We can also shorten the command to `docker image ls *nginx`. It yields the same result.

Let's tag the image. We will tag `my-nginx` to `127.0.0.1:5000/my-nginx` so it can be pushed into our private Docker registry. We can do this using the `docker image tag` command (`docker tag` for the old-style, top-level command):

```
$ docker image tag my-nginx 127.0.0.1:5000/my-nginx
```

We can check using `image ls` again to see that the `tag` command is done successfully:

```
$ docker image ls 127.0.0.1:5000/my-nginx
REPOSITORY                TAG       IMAGE ID      CREATED      SIZE
127.0.0.1:5000/my-nginx   latest    a773a4303694  1 days ago   216MB
```

OK, that looks great! We can now push the `my-nginx` image to the local repository, of course with `docker image push`, and the process will be very quick because the Docker repository is locally here on our machine.

 Again, you will find that the hash number is not the same as in the following listing when you try the commands. It is harmless; please just ignore it.

Now, execute the following command to push the `my-nginx` image onto the local private repository:

```
$ docker image push 127.0.0.1:5000/my-nginx
The push refers to a repository [127.0.0.1:5000/my-nginx]
b3c96f2520ad: Pushed
a09947e71dc0: Pushed
9c42c2077cde: Pushed
625c7a2a783b: Pushed
25e0901a71b8: Pushed
8aa4fcad5eeb: Pushed
latest: digest: sha256:c69c400a56b43db695 ... size: 1569
```

The hard part has already been done beautifully. We now go back to the simple part: pushing an image to Docker Hub. Before we continue, please sign up for your Docker ID at `https://hub.docker.com/` if you don't have one yet.

To store an image there, we have to tag the image with the `<docker id>/<image name>` format. For pushing `my-nginx` to the Docker Hub, we will `image tag` it to `<docker id>/my-nginx`. I'll use my Docker ID there. Replace `<docker id>` with your registered Docker ID:

```
$ docker image tag my-nginx chanwit/my-nginx
```

Before pushing, we need to log in to the Docker Hub first using the `docker login` command. Please use `-u` and your Docker ID to specify the account. We will be asked for a password; if everything is OK, the command will say `Login Succeeded`:

```
$ docker login -u chanwit
Password:
Login Succeeded
```

Please note that our username and password are insecurely stored in `~/.docker/config.json`, so please do not forget to type `docker logout` whenever possible.

Running a container

Now, let us run a container from our `my-nginx` image. We will use the `docker container run` command (the old, top-level command is `docker run`). This is done to run our container as a background process with `-d` and bind port `8080` of the host to port `80` of the container (`-p 8080:80`). We specified the container name with `--name`. If we run the container successfully, we will get a hash number, starting with `4382d778bcc9` in this example. It is the ID of our running container:

```
$ docker container run --name=my-nginx -d -p 8080:80 my-nginx
4382d778bcc96f70dd290e8ef9454d5a260e87366eadbd1060c7b6e087b3df26
```

Open the web browser and point it to `http://localhost:8080`; we will see the NGINX server running:

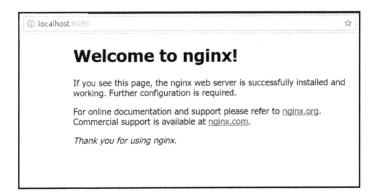

Figure 2.5: Example of NGINX running inside a container

Now our NGINX server is running as a background container serving on the host's `8080` port. We can use the `docker container ls` command (or the old-style, top-level `docker ps`) to list all running containers:

```
$ docker container ls
CONTAINER ID   IMAGE       COMMAND               CREATED         ...
4382d778bcc9   my-nginx    "nginx -g 'daemon ..." 2 seconds ago  ...
6f7dc5ef89f0   registry:2  "/entrypoint.sh /e..." 2 hours ago    ...
```

We can control the life cycle of the container using the commands `docker container start`, `stop`, `pause`, or `kill`, for example.

If we would like to force removal of running containers, we can use `docker container rm -f <container id or name>` to do so. Let's remove all running instances of `my-nginx` and the private registry before continuing to play around with a Docker Swarm cluster:

```
$ docker container rm -f my-nginx registry
my-nginx
registry
```

Docker Swarm clusters

A cluster is a group of machines connecting together to do work. A Docker host is a physical or virtual machine with the Docker Engine installed. We create a Docker Swarm cluster by connecting many Docker hosts together. We refer to each Docker host as a Docker Swarm node, simply a node.

In version 1.12, Docker introduced Swarm mode, a new orchestration engine to replace the old Swarm cluster, which is now referred to as **Swarm classic**. The main difference between Swarm classic and Swarm mode is that Swarm classic uses an external service, such as Consul, etcd, or Apache ZooKeeper as its key/value store, but Swarm mode has this key/value built in. With this, Swarm mode keeps orchestration latency at a minimum, and is more robust than Swarm classic because it does not need to interact with an external store. The monolithic nature of Swarm mode is good for making changes to its algorithms. For example, one of my research works implemented the Ant Colony optimization to improve how Swarm placing containers ran on non-uniform clusters.

From experiments at our laboratory, we have found that Swarm classic has limitations when scaling to 100–200 nodes. With Swarm mode, we have done experiments with the Docker community to show that it can scale to at least 4,700 nodes.

The results are publicly available at project Swarm2K (`https://github.com/swarmzilla/swarm2k`) and Swarm3K (`https://github.com/swarmzilla/swarm3k`) on GitHub.

The key to the performance of Swarm mode is that it is built on top of the embedded *etcd* library. The embedded etcd library provides a mechanism for storing the state of a cluster in a distributed fashion. All state information is maintained in the Raft logs database with the Raft consensus algorithm.

In this section, we discuss how to set up a cluster in Swarm mode.

Setting up a cluster

To create a fully functional single-node Swarm cluster, we just type the following command:

```
$ docker swarm init
Swarm initialized: current node (jbl2cz9gkilvu5i6ahtxlkypa) is now a
manager.
To add a worker to this swarm, run the following command:
    docker swarm join --token
SWMTKN-1-470wlqyqbsxhk6gps0o9597izmsjx4xeht5cy3df5sc9nu5n6u-9vlvcxjv5jjrcps
4trjcocaae 192.168.1.4:2377
To add a manager to this swarm, run 'docker swarm join-token manager' and
follow the instructions.
```

We call this process Swarm cluster initialization. This process initializes the new cluster by preparing the `/var/lib/docker/swarm` directory to store all states related to the cluster. Here's the contents of `/var/lib/docker/swarm`, which could be backed up if needed:

```
$ sudo ls -al /var/lib/docker/swarm

total 28
drwx------  5  root root 4096 Sep 30 23:31 .
drwx--x--x 12  root root 4096 Sep 29 15:23 ..
drwxr-xr-x  2  root root 4096 Sep 30 23:31 certificates
-rw-------  1  root root 124  Sep 30 23:31 docker-state.json
drwx------  4  root root 4096 Sep 30 23:31 raft
-rw-------  1  root root 67   Sep 30 23:31 state.json
drwxr-xr-x  2  root root 4096 Sep 30 23:31 worker
```

If we have many network interfaces on the host, the previous command will fail as Docker Swarm requires us to specify an advertised address using an IP address, or a certain network interface.

In the following example, I use my `wlan0` IP address as the advertised address of the cluster. This means that any machine on the Wi-Fi network can try to join this cluster:

```
$ docker swarm init --advertise-addr=192.168.1.4:2377
```

Similarly, we may advertise using the name of a network interface, for example, `eth0`:

```
$ docker swarm init --advertise-addr=eth0
```

Choose the style that works best for your working environment.

After initialization, we get a fully working, single-node cluster. To force a node to leave the current cluster, we use the following command:

```
$ docker swarm leave --force
Node left the swarm.
```

If we run this command on a single-node cluster, the cluster will be destroyed. If you run the preceding command here, please do not forget to initialize the cluster again with `docker swarm init` before proceeding to the next section.

Masters and workers

Recall that we used the term Docker host to refer to a machine with Docker installed. When we join these hosts together to form a cluster, sometimes we call each of them a Docker node.

A Swarm cluster consists of two kinds of Docker nodes, a master and a worker. We say node `mg0` has the master role, and node `w01` has the worker role, for example. We form a cluster by joining other nodes to a master, usually the first master. The `docker swarm join` command requires the security tokens to be different, to allow a node to join as the master or as the worker. Please note that we must run the `docker swarm join` command on each node, not on the master node:

```
# Login to each node
$ docker swarm join --token
SWMTKN-1-27uhz2azpesmsxu0t1li2e2uhdr2hudn3e2x5afilc02x1zicc-9wd3glqr5i92xmx
vpnzdwz2j9 192.168.1.4:2377
```

A master node is responsible for controlling the cluster. The best practice recommended by Docker is that odd numbers of master nodes are the best configurations. We should have an odd number of master nodes starting from three. If we have three masters, one of them is allowed to fail and the cluster will still work.

The following table shows the possible configurations, from one to six master nodes. For example, a cluster of three master nodes allows one master to fail and it still maintains the cluster. If two masters fail, the cluster will not be allowed to operate, starting or stopping services. However, in that state, the running containers will not die and continue to run:

Master nodes	Number of masters to maintain cluster	Failed masters allowed
1	1	0
2	2	0
3 (best)	2	1
4	3	1
5 (best)	3	2
6	4	2

The best option to recover the cluster after losing the majority of master nodes is to bring the failed master nodes back online as fast as possible.

In the production cluster, we usually do not schedule running *tasks* on master nodes. A master node needs to have enough CPU, memory, and network bandwidth to properly handle node information and Raft logs. We control the cluster by commanding one of the master nodes. For example, we can list all nodes of a cluster by sending the following command to a master:

```
$ docker node ls

ID              HOSTNAME  STATUS  AVAILABILITY  MANAGER STATUS
wbb8rb0xob *    mg0       Ready   Active        Leader
```

What we see in the result is the list of all nodes in the current cluster. We can tell that the mg0 node is a manager by looking at the MANAGER STATUS column. If a manager node is the primary manager of the cluster, MANAGER STATUS will say it is a Leader. If we have two more manager nodes here, the status will tell us they are a Follower. Here's how this leader/follower mechanism works. When we issue a command to the leader, the leader performs the command and the state of the cluster is changed. The cluster state is then updated by also sending this change to other manager nodes, that is, followers. If we issue a command to a follower, it will forward the command to the leader instead of doing that itself. Basically, all commands for the cluster will be performed by the leader, and the followers will update the changes to their internal Raft logs only.

If a new manager node would like to join, we require a master token for it. Type the docker swarm join-token manager command to obtain a security token to join a cluster in a manager role:

```
$ docker swarm join-token manager

To add a manager to this swarm, run the following command:

    docker swarm join --token
SWMTKN-1-2c6finlm9d97q075kpwxcn59q93vbpfaf5qp13awjin3s3jopw-5hex62dfsd3360z
xds46i6s56 192.168.1.4:2377
```

Although a task as a container can be running on both kinds of nodes, we usually do not submit tasks to run on master nodes. We only use worker nodes to run tasks in production. To join worker nodes to the cluster, we pass the worker token to the join command. Use docker swarm join-token worker to obtain a worker token.

Services and tasks

Along with the new orchestration engine, Docker introduced the new abstraction of services and tasks in version 1.12. A service may consist of many instances of a task. We call each instance a replica. Each instance of a task runs on a Docker node in the form of a container.

A service can be created using the following command:

```
$ docker service create \
    --replicas 3 \
    --name web \
    -p 80:80 \
    --constraint node.role==worker \
    nginx
```

This web service consists of three tasks, specified with `--replicas`. These tasks are submitted by the orchestration engine to run on selected nodes. The service's name, web, can be resolved using a virtual IP address. Other services on the same network, in this case maybe a reverse proxy service, can refer to it. We use `--name` to specify the name of the service.

We continue the discussion of the details of this command in the following diagram:

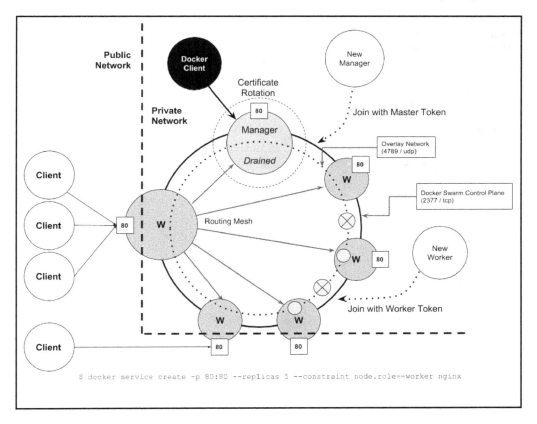

Figure 2.6: Swarm cluster in action

We assume that our cluster consists of one manager node and five worker nodes. There is no high availability setup for the manager; this will be left as an exercise for the reader.

We start at the manager. The manager is set to be *drained* because we do not want it to accept any scheduled tasks. This is the best practice, and we can drain a node as follows:

```
$ docker node update --availability drain mg0
```

This service will be published to port 80 on the routing mesh. The routing mesh is a mechanism to perform load balancing inside the Swarm mode. Port 80 will be opened on every worker node to serve this service. When a request comes in, the routing mesh will route the request to a certain container (a task) on a certain node, automatically.

The routing mesh relies on a Docker network with the overlay driver, namely `ingress`. We can use `docker network ls` to list all active networks:

```
$ docker network ls
NETWORK ID      NAME              DRIVER    SCOPE
c32139129f45    bridge            bridge    local
3315d809348e    docker_gwbridge   bridge    local
90103ae1188f    host              host      local
ve7fj61ifakr    ingress           overlay   swarm
489d441af28d    none              null      local
```

We find a network with ID `ve7fj61ifakr` which is an `overlay` network of the `swarm` scope. As the information implies, this kind of network is working only in Docker Swarm mode. To see the details of this network, we use the `docker network inspect ingress` command:

```
$ docker network inspect ingress
[
    {
        "Name": "ingress",
        "Id": "ve7fj61ifakr8ybux1icawwbr",
        "Created": "2017-10-02T23:22:46.72494239+07:00",
        "Scope": "swarm",
        "Driver": "overlay",
        "EnableIPv6": false,
        "IPAM": {
            "Driver": "default",
            "Options": null,
            "Config": [
                {
                    "Subnet": "10.255.0.0/16",
                    "Gateway": "10.255.0.1"
                }
            ]
        },
    }
]
```

We can see that the `ingress` network has a subnet of 10.255.0.0/16, which means that we are allowed to use 65,536 IP addresses in this network by default. This number is the maximum number of tasks (containers) created by `docker service create -p` on a single Swarm mode cluster. This number is not affected when we use `docker container run -p` outside the Swarm.

To create a Swarm scoped overlay network, we use the `docker network create` command:

```
$ docker network create  --driver overlay appnet
1u29kfat35xph3beilupcw4m2

$ docker network ls
NETWORK ID      NAME               DRIVER     SCOPE
1u29kfat35xp    appnet             overlay    swarm
c32139129f45    bridge             bridge     local
3315d809348e    docker_gwbridge    bridge     local
90103ae1188f    host               host       local
ve7fj61ifakr    ingress            overlay    swarm
489d441af28d    none               null       local
```

We can check again with the `docker network ls` command and see the `appnet` network with the `overlay` driver and `swarm` scope there. Your network's ID will be different. To attach a service to a specific network, we can pass the network name to the `docker service create` command. For example:

```
$ docker service create --name web --network appnet -p 80:80 nginx
```

The preceding example creates the `web` service and attaches it to the `appnet` network. This command works if, and only if, the appnet is Swarm-scoped.

We can dynamically detach or re-attach net networks to the current running service using the `docker service update` command with `--network-add` or `--network-rm`, respectively. Try the following command:

```
$ docker service update --network-add appnet web
web
```

Here, we can observe the result with `docker inspect web`. You will find a chunk of JSON printed out with the last block looking as follows:

```
$ docker inspect web

    . . .
```

```
        "UpdateStatus": {
            "State": "completed",
            "StartedAt": "2017-10-09T15:45:03.413491944Z",
            "CompletedAt": "2017-10-09T15:45:21.155296293Z",
            "Message": "update completed"
        }
    }
]
```

It means that the service has been updated and the process of updating has been completed. We will now have the web service attaching to the appnet network:

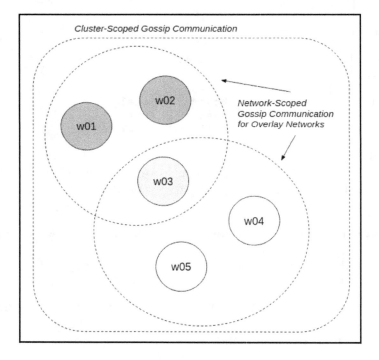

Figure 2.7: The Gossip communication mechanism for Swarm-scope overlay networks

Overlay networks rely on the **gossip** protocol implementation over port 7946, for both TCP and UDP, accompanied by Linux's VXLAN over UDP port 4789. The overlay network is implemented with performance in mind. A network will cover only the necessary hosts and gradually expand when needed.

We can scale a service by increasing or decreasing the number of its replicas. Scaling the service can be done using the `docker service scale` command. For example, if we would like to scale the `web` service to five replicas, we could issue the following command:

```
$ docker service scale web=5
```

When the service is scaled, and its task is scheduled on a new node, all related networks bound to this service will be expanded to cover the new node automatically. In the following diagram, we have two replicas of the app service, and we would like to scale it from two to three with the command `docker service scale app=3`. The new replica **app.3** will be scheduled on the worker node **w03**. Then the overlay network bound to this app service will be expanded to cover node **w03** too. The network-scoped gossip communication is responsible for the network expansion mechanism:

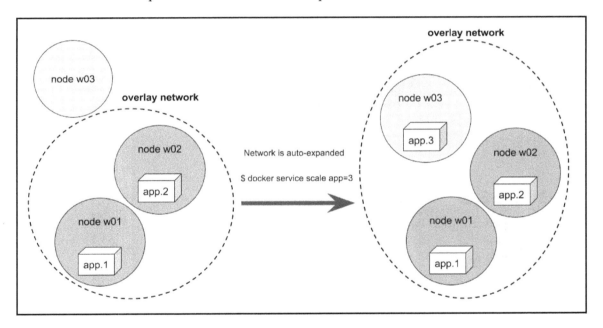

Figure 2.8: Swarm-scoped network expansion

Docker and serverless

How will Docker benefit us? When dealing with application development, Docker can be used to simplify the development toolchain. We can pack everything we need to write serverless applications into a single container image and let the whole team use it. This ensures consistency of tool versions and ensures they will not mess up our development machines.

We will then use Docker to prepare our infrastructure. Actually, the term serverless means developers should not maintain their own infrastructure. However, in cases where the public cloud is not an option, we can use Docker to simplify infrastructure provisioning. Using the same architecture as the third-party serverless platforms on our company's infrastructure, we can minimize the operation and maintenance costs. Later chapters will discuss how we can operate our own Docker-based FaaS infrastructure.

For the serverless application itself, we use Docker as a wrapper for serverless functions. We use Docker as a unit of work, so that any kind of binary can be integrated into our serverless platform, ranging from the legacy COBOL, C, or Pascal programs to the programs written in modern languages, such as Node.js, Kotlin, or Crystal. In the 17.06+ versions of Docker, it is also possible to form a Swarm cluster across multi-hardware architecture. We can even host Windows-based C# functions on the same cluster as mainframe-based COBOL programs.

Exercises

To help you better remember and understand the concepts and practices of Docker described in this chapter, try answering the following questions without going back to the chapter's contents. Let's get started:

1. What are containers? What's the key difference between containers and virtual machines?
2. What are the main features inside the Linux kernel to enable container technology? Please name at least two of them.
3. What are the key concepts of the Docker workflow?
4. What is a Dockerfile for? Which Docker command do you use to interact with it?
5. What is the ENTRYPOINT instruction inside a Dockerfile?
6. Which command do we use to list all Docker images?

7. Which command do we use to form a Docker Swarm cluster?
8. What is the key difference between Swarm classic and Swarm mode?
9. Please explain the relationship between services and tasks.
10. How can we create an NGINX service with five replicas?
11. How can we scale down the number of the NGINX services to two?
12. What is the minimum number of nodes required to form a Swarm cluster with the high-availability property? Why?
13. What is the name for a network that is part of the routing mesh? How large is it?
14. Which port numbers are used by a Swarm cluster? What are they for?
15. What is the main benefit of network-scoped Gossip communication?

Summary

This chapter started off by discussing the concepts of containers. Then we reviewed what Docker is, how to install it, and the Docker build, ship, and run workflow. We then learnt how to form a Docker Swarm cluster and Swarm master and worker nodes. We learnt how to properly set up a robust Swarm cluster with an odd number of master nodes. We then learnt the service and task concepts of Docker Swarm. Finally, we learnt how Docker fits into serverless application development.

In the next chapter, we will review serverless frameworks and platforms to understand the overall architecture and the limitations of them.

3
Serverless Frameworks

This chapter discusses serverless frameworks. What are they? What are the current limitations of pure serverless frameworks? How could Docker partially solve the limitations of serverless frameworks. We will start by taking a look at AWS Lambda, then Azure Functions, and Google Cloud Functions. We will touch briefly on IBM Cloud Functions, but actually its engine is OpenWhisk, which will be discussed in detail in the next couple of chapters.

We will also discuss serverless framework, a toolkit that helps us develop cloud-independent serverless applications, in the last section of this chapter.

AWS Lambda

Among serverless architectures offered by cloud providers, AWS Lambda is the most popular and has some advanced features.

FaaS/serverless is a natural evolution from microservices, or we may think of it as an extension to the microservices architecture. In many scenarios, we can complement our microservices architecture with functions or Lambda. If you are already an AWS customer, it is completely natural to move your codes from EC2 to Lambda and save a lot of money. The following diagram illustrates a simple use case that uses **AWS Lambda** together with **S3 Buckets** and **DynamoDB**:

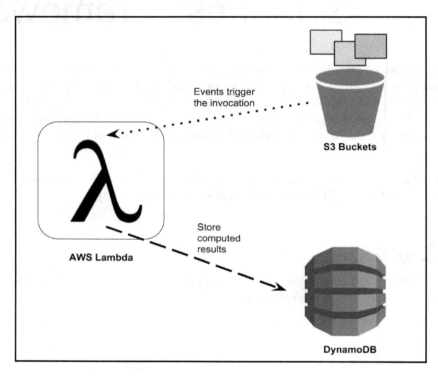

Figure 3.1: A simple use case of using Lambda function on AWS

In S3, there is a way to trigger the event to a specific endpoint. We put the endpoint of our Lambda function there. After users upload or make changes to the S3 bucket, it will trigger to send an invocation request to the Lambda function. This could be thought of as a form of WebHooks. After that, the Lambda function receives the event and starts to compute its application logic. After it has finished, the Lambda will transfer the results and store them into a DynamoDB instance.

We will demonstrate a similar scenario in Chapter 8, *Putting Them All Together*.

Limitations

Lambda supports several language runtimes; for example, Node.js, Go, Java, Python, and C#. Each AWS Lambda has a number of limitations to cap the resources it may use per invocation. In terms of memory, the range of RAM supported for Lambda is between 128 MB to 3,008 MB with 64 MB, increments. The function will be automatically terminated if its memory usage is exceeded.

In terms of disk space, a Lambda function is allowed to use the /tmp directory up to 512 MB. This kind of disk volume is ephemeral, so it is expected to be wiped out after the Lambda has finished its work. Also, the number of file descriptors allowed in Lambda functions are limited to 1,024, while the number of processes and threads that could be forked within a single invocation is limited to 1,024 as well.

For each request, the size of the request body is capped at 6 MB for synchronous HTTP calls, and at 128 KB for asynchronous, event-triggered calls.

The most important aspect here is *time limits*. AWS Lambda allows a function to run no longer than 5 minutes (or 300 seconds). If the execution time exceeds 5 minutes, the function will be automatically killed.

Lambda termination

The technology behind Lambda is actually container-based, which means it isolates a function from other instances. The container's sandbox provides resources specific to each configuration for them.

A Lambda function can be terminated in a number of ways:

- **Timeout**: As previously mentioned, when the 5-minute limitation is reached, the current execution of the function will be stopped no matter what it is doing.
- **Controlled termination**: If the function provides a callback and the callback is executed to invoke the context.done() method, the function will be terminated, no matter what it is doing.
- **Default termination**: The function ends and terminates normally. Also, there is no callback to invoke the context.done() method. This case will be considered as the default termination.
- **Function crashes or process.exit() is called**: If the function panics or generates segmentation faults, the function will terminate and therefore the container is stopped.

Container reuse

There is a scenario where the function container that has just terminated could be reused.

This ability to reuse a finished function container can greatly reduce the spinning up time, as the initialization process will be completely skipped. Also, there is a drawback where, if a container is reused, the file written to the /tmp directory from the previous execution may still be there.

Native executables

Lambda is actually designed to run code in any language, as Lambda's sandbox is just a container. The trick is that we could use a Node.js program to execute any binary shipped with the ZIP file before uploading.

It is worth noting that when preparing our own binary for Lambda, it must be statically compiled or matched with the shared libraries provided by Amazon Linux (as the containers used on Lambda are all Amazon Linux-based). It is our responsibility to track the Amazon Linux version by ourselves.

A project such as LambCI (http://github.com/lambci/docker-lambda) can help to solve this problem. LambCI provides a local sandbox environment, as Docker containers, that mimics the AWS Lambda environment by installing the same software and libraries, file structure, and permissions. It also defines the same set of environment variables, and other behaviors. Also, the username and group are defined to match the Lambda, for example, sbx_user1051.

With this local environment, we are allowed to safely test our codes inside this Docker container and can be sure that it will be running fine on Lambda.

Azure Functions

Azure Functions is a serverless computing platform offered by Microsoft as a part of Azure Cloud. All design goals are the same as other serverless/FaaS services, and Azure Functions enables us to execute our application logic without managing our own infrastructure.

Azure Functions runs a program in the form of scripts when it is triggered by events. The current version of Azure Functions supports language runtimes such as C#, F#, PHP, Node.js or Java. It is natural for Azure to support C# and F# as first-class languages for their functions because they are Microsoft-owned programming languages. In any case, the only GA-supported languages are C#, F#, and JavaScript (Node.js) anyway.

With C#, F#, or .NET languages, Azure Functions allows us to install dependencies via NuGet, the infamous package manager for .NET. In case we are writing JavaScript with Node.js, Azure also provides access to NPM for package management.

Similar to other cloud providers, Azure Functions has an advantage when accessing other Azure services, for example, Azure Cosmos DB, Azure Event Hubs, Azure Storage and Azure Service Bus.

It is really interesting to note that the pricing model of Azure Functions is somewhat different from the offering of Amazon or Google. In Azure, there are two kind of pricing plans that may fit different needs.

The first one is the *consumption plan*. It is a similar plan offered by other cloud providers, where you pay only for the time that our codes are executed. The second one is the *app service plan*. Functions in this context are considered part of the app service for other applications. If functions fall into this category, we do not need to incur additional cost.

An interesting feature of Azure Functions is its triggering and binding mechanism. Azure Functions allows a definition of how to trigger a function and how to perform data binding of the input and the output for each function, in a separated configuration. These mechanisms help to avoid hardcoding when we call functions and when we transform data in and out through the calling chain of functions.

Scaling

In Azure, there is a component to monitor the number of requests made to each Azure Function in real time. This component is called the **scale controller**. It collects data and then later makes a decision to scale the number of instances up or down for that function. Azure has the concept of an app service. A function app may contain many instances of a function.

All decision making is based on heuristic-based algorithms for different types of event triggers. When the function is scaled out, all resources related to that function will also be scaled out. The number of function instances will be automatically scaled down to zero, if there is no request made to the function app.

Limitations

Each function instance will be limited to a memory of 1.5 GB by the host of the function app, a group-like semantic for multiple function instances. All functions within a function app share the same resources.

A function app holds a maximum of 200 instances of a function at the same time. But there is no concurrency limitation. In practice, a function instance can accept one or more requests.

 Each event trigger, for example, Azure Service Bus has its own heuristic way to scale the underlying function.

Durable functions

One of the most advanced extensions to the Azure Functions are **durable functions**. A durable function is a technique to implement stateful functions inside a serverless computing environment. There are additional concepts for state management, checkpoints, and restarts provided by this durable extension. What we get from this kind of function is a stateful workflow, and there will be a driver that acts as the orchestrator to call other functions, as shown in the following diagram:

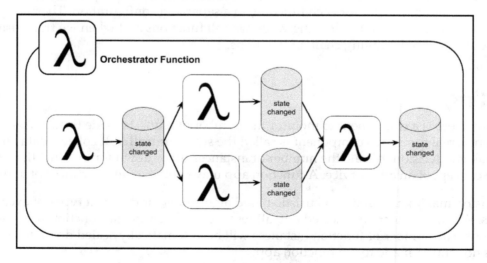

Figure 3.2: An orchestrator function with the durable function extension in Azure

When it has finished calling other functions, both in synchronous or asynchronous ways, the orchestrator function will be allowed to save states as local variables. There is also a *checkpointing technique* to continue/resume the orchestrator's states when the calling process has to start over, or the virtual machine running this orchestrator function gets rebooted.

Google Cloud Functions

The serverless computing service offered by Google Inc is called **Google Cloud Functions (GCF)**.

We basically refer to it as GCF in this section. Like other serverless platforms, GCF provides both execution environment and the SDK to help us develop and manage the entire life cycle of our function. It provides an SDK to help us get started with the framework. The main language supported by GCF is JavaScript and there is a Node.js Docker image for us to use. With Docker, it is convenient to build a function. When about to deploy, it is relatively easy to deploy it with the Google Cloud CLI tool. It is natural that GCF will allow us to connect to other Google-based services efficiently:

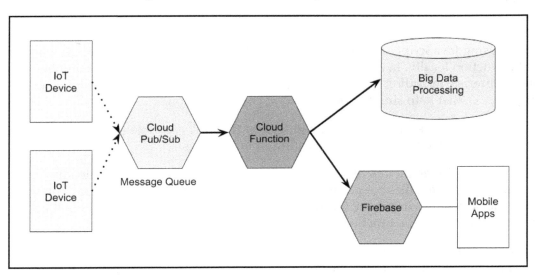

Figure 3.3: A common IoT use case implemented with Google Cloud Functions

The preceding diagram demonstrates one of the common use cases implemented on Google Cloud. It is an example of an IoT pipeline using all Google Cloud services. A Google Cloud Function is used to compute data from the message queue and divert it to both the big data stack and Firebase. The Firebase service acts as a **Backend as a Service (BaaS)** for mobile applications. In a later chapter, we will demonstrate a similar BaaS using the **Parse platform**.

Overview

The definition of a function in the FaaS or the serverless platform is that it should focus on only one objective. Due to the nature of the function, it should not be too complex. As we described in Chapter 1, *Serverless and Docker*, serverless FaaS is actually a subset of the event-driven programming model. All cloud functions on GCF behave that way. Every single component of our application pipeline is connected by sending events to another. Also, events can be monitored. When we receive an event from the source, a cloud function associated with that mechanism will be triggered to run.

The function supported by GCF must be written in JavaScript, or languages that are able to transpile to JavaScript. At the time of writing, the environment for executing functions is a Node.js v6.11.5. Basically, developers would use any Node.js runtime that matches the same version. Using JavaScript and Node.js yields good portability and it allows developers to test the function locally. In addition, using Node.js allows access to the vast numbers of Node.js libraries, including APIs offered by the platform (https://cloud.google.com/nodejs/apis), that help simplify development and integration.

GCF is designed to be a connection or a glue layer that links services together. In some use cases, we use functions to extend the existing cloud services.

With the event-driven model, functions can listen and wait until the file uploading event is triggered, when some files are put into cloud storage. We can also listen to log changing in a remote blockchain environment. Or maybe we subscribe to a Pub/Sub topics and get a notification to trigger the functions.

We usually put some complex business logic inside a function. Cloud functions owned by Google have the ability to access the credential system of the GCP, therefore, it could authenticate with the large set of GCP services. This feature usually makes the cloud functions very useful on their own platform.

All infrastructure and the system software layers are fully managed by Google's platform, so we need to care only for our codes. Autoscaling is also the normal feature of this kind of platform. Provisioning additional computing resources just works automatically when the number of triggers becomes large. Deployed functions will autoscale to serve millions of requests without any further configuration from us.

The fine-grained concept of an FaaS function makes this kind of computing fit nicely to implement self-contained APIs and WebHooks (we will demonstrate this in later chapters). Google Cloud Functions supports many aspects of workloads, for example, data processing/ELT, WebHooks, implementing APIs, acting as a backend for mobile applications, and accepting streaming data from IoT devices.

GCF supports many aspects of serverless computing. An obvious limitation at the moment is that it supports only Node.js as a programming language. GCF uses containers internally to wrap around the Node.js codes and deploy onto its internal orchestration FaaS system. A part of this engineering has been open sourced as a project called **distroless**. We can accomplish similar things with the concept of declarative containers, proposed in the final chapter. Using this concept allows us to deploy a workload containing only the application in the same way GCF does.

All of these use cases allowed by GCF will be demonstrated with different approaches using Docker and FaaS platforms in a later chapter.

Execution model

Google takes care of everything for us, including the hardware level, the OS, networking, and the application runtimes. A function deployed there on the GCF will run in an automatically managed platform. Each cloud function will be executed separately in a container-based isolation, which is a secure execution context. Running independently, each function will not interfere with others while sharing the same host. This is the same concept used by Docker and other container implementations.

At the time of writing, Google Cloud Functions chooses to support only JavaScript running on Node.js v6.11.5; however, the document says that they will keep the version of Node.js updated by going closely with the **Long-Term Support** (**LTS**) releases, as quickly as possible. We can be confident that all patch versions for security and minor updates of the Node.js runtime will match the upstream releases.

As previously mentioned, a cloud function is also put into a container. In the case of Google Cloud Functions, its root filesystem is based on *Debian*. The base image of GCF is updated regularly and available as Docker images. It could be pulled from `gcr.io/google-appengine/nodejs`. Here's the way the system prepares the base image by inheriting the image and installing Node.js version 6.11.5 to it:

```
FROM gcr.io/google-appengine/nodejs
RUN install_node v6.11.5
```

Statelessness

Stateless is the preferred model when writing a serverless FaaS function. Why? Because in the fully managed execution environment, which can be scaled up and down at anytime, we cannot expect our function state to be preserved. So it is best to not save anything to the function's local storage. If we need memory, such as global variables that may be shared across instances of the function, these variables must be managed explicitly by external storage services.

In some situations, saying a function is completely stateless makes us underutilize the execution context of that function. As we already know, our function is actually running inside a container isolation. And it is completely fine for our function to write some things onto the local storage during execution, of course, without the expectation to share states outside this isolation. When saying *stateless* in the container's context, it is likely to be the *share-nothing* model rather than being *stateless*. The share-nothing model, is the better word to generally describe the statelessness of container-based FaaS.

Timeout

In general, a serverless platform usually caps the execution time of a cloud function to prevent overuse of the platform's computing resources. For Google Cloud Functions, the default timeout is set to be 1 minute and can be extended to 9 minutes if the user prefers. When a function is timed out, its running codes are terminated. For example, if a function is scheduled to run at the 3 minutes after it starts, and if the timeout is set to be 2, that function will never run.

Execution guarantees

An error can occur anytime during the execution of a function. A function might not be executed only once if it failed. The model of execution depends on the type of function.

For example, a simple synchronous HTTP request will be invoked once, at most. This means that the function invocation will be failed and never retried. The caller side is responsible for error handling and the retry strategy on its own.

While asynchronous functions will be invoked at least once, as is the nature of these asynchronous calls, so we need to prepare for a situation that this kind of function will be invoked multiple times. Also, the state to be modified by these functions should be idempotent and robust. For example, we may need to implement a state machine to control the states of the system.

IBM Cloud Functions

IBM Cloud Functions is a service provided by IBM Cloud. It is powered by Apache OpenWhisk; actually, it's IBM who donated OpenWhisk to the Apache Foundation. We have a chapter dedicated to OpenWhisk later in this book.

The Cloud Functions service provided by IBM is, of course, very similar to other function services in terms of concepts. Functions wrap around the application business logic and run in the event-driven FaaS environment managed by IBM.

Functions are designed to respond to a direct HTTP invocation from other Web or mobile apps, or to events triggered by other supported systems, for example, Cloudant. IBM Cloud provides Cloudant, a commercially supported JSON data store built on top of CouchDB. We can prepare a trigger in the Cloudant system, and let it fire events to invoke functions defined in the IBM Cloud Functions, when the data in Cloudant is changed.

The design goal of functions is generally the same among cloud providers. They provide a way for us developers to focus only on writing application business logic, then uploading codes to their cloud as cloud functions.

To further explore the concepts behind OpenWhisk, the engine behind IBM Cloud, please feel free to jump to `Chapter 6`, *OpenWhisk on Docker*, to learn more about OpenWhisk.

The Serverless Framework

The Serverless Framework is an application development framework and tool for the serverless computing paradigm. The framework only shares the same name with serverless. Please do not be confused.

The authors of the Serverless Framework consider that a serverless application is the next evolution of application development in the cloud native ecosystem. And this kind of application needs a certain level of automation. This idea was the stem of the framework.

The design idea views managed services and functions as coupled entities. To make an application around them, a tool should provide build, test, and deploy commands to make the whole development life cycle fully automated.

There also should be a consistent way of building, testing, and deploying a serverless application to multiple cloud providers, while minimizing code changes. The framework should help configure the setting for each cloud provider based on the following:

- The language runtime
- The cloud provider selected by the application developer

With this level of abstraction, the framework yields real advantages and lets developers focus on application business logic, rather than keep changing cloud configurations to match each provider.

There are four benefits of the Serverless Framework described by its creators:

- The Serverless Framework helps speed up the development process because the framework contains CLI-based commands to create a project, build, and also helps to test applications from the same development environment. It saves time because the Serverless Framework is independent from any cloud providers. There is also a mechanism to deploy a new version to the cloud and allow rollback for the previous one, if it fails.
- With the Serverless Framework, it allows us to develop codes independently to any cloud providers. So, the code with a good writing style would be migrated across the providers. For example, we can simply move our functions deployed as AWS Lambda by just changing the provider in the YAML file to Google Cloud and re-deploy again. But actually this is only a part of the whole problem. It is actually not the codes that could lock you to the vendor, it's the services provided by the vendor that make you stay with them. So choose the supported service wisely and this problem could be effectively solved.
- The Serverless Framework helps to enable **Infrastructure as Code** (**IaC**). With deployment that could be done via the set of APIs, we enable a certain level of automation. This makes us able to fully deploy the system as multi-cloud applications.

- Finally, the framework is widely used and has a very vibrant community. This is also an important key for choosing a tool. The framework extensions are actively developed by the community because of the base language, JavaScript on Node.js, that they chose for the framework. So, it is relatively easy to add a new provider to the framework. A notable community-based provider is Kubeless.

Exercise

Let's do some revision by trying to answer the questions without reviewing the contents:

1. How long is the time limitation for an AWS Lambda?
2. Why do you think the cloud providers limit computational time for FaaS functions?
3. What are Azure's durable functions? Do they have any benefit?
4. How can we test an AWS Lambda program just with Docker?
5. What's the engine behind IBM Cloud Functions? What do you think is the reason behind IBM open sourcing it?
6. What is the Serverless Framework? Why is it important?
7. How could we make a FaaS function work across cloud providers? Do you think it is really possible?
8. Please explain the difference between stateless and share-nothing models.

Summary

In this section, we have discussed four major serverless computing platforms, some of their characteristics and limitations. We have also discussed the Serverless Framework, a framework and tool designed to help build, test, and deploy applications to multiple serverless computing platforms.

In the next three chapters, we will see the truly different aspects of the serverless platforms provided by cloud providers and serverless/FaaS platforms that allow us to deploy them on our own with Docker technologies.

4
OpenFaaS on Docker

This chapter will introduce OpenFaaS, a serverless framework that uses a software container as a unit of deployment. OpenFaaS has been designed to run and utilize the orchestration engine in Docker Swarm mode.

The chapter will start by introducing OpenFaaS and explaining its architecture. Then we will go on to discuss how to use OpenFaaS to prepare and deploy functions. Finally, this chapter will end with how to install a Grafana/Prometheus dashboard for OpenFaaS.

What is OpenFaaS?

OpenFaaS is a framework and infrastructure preparation system for building serverless applications. It originated from the serverless framework in the Docker Swarm and now supports other kinds of infrastructure backends, such as Kubernetes or Hyper.sh. Functions in OpenFaaS are containers. Any program written in any language can be packed as a function by leveraging the container technologies of Docker. This enables us to fully reuse the existing code to consume a wide range of web service events without rewriting the code. OpenFaaS is a great tool for modernizing old systems to run on a cloud-based infrastructure.

There are several serverless frameworks out there in the cloud-native landscape. However, some problems need to be addressed by Alex Ellis, the original author of OpenFaaS. The driving factor behind the making of the framework is shaping the following, compelling features:

- **Ease of use**: Basically, many serverless frameworks are complex to deploy by nature, as they are built by big companies and are serverless services. OpenFaaS, on the other hand, aims to be a serverless stack that is easy enough for developers and small companies to deploy and use on their own hardware. OpenFaaS also comes with a ready-to-use UI portal, which allows us to try out function invocation in the browser. OpenFaaS has autoscaling capability built in. It measures the load of function invocation automatically and scales instances up or down on demand.

- **Portable**: There are several orchestration engines in the container ecosystem, notably Docker Swarm and Google's Kubernetes. OpenFaaS was first designed to work on Swarm and later on Kubernetes. Its functions are portable across these orchestration engines. Not only portable in a runtime sense, an OpenFaaS function is just a plain Docker container. This means that every kind of workload can be repacked as a function container and simply deployed on an OpenFaaS cluster. OpenFaaS runs on any infrastructure, including on-premises hardware, private clouds, and public clouds.

- **Simplicity in architecture and design**: The architecture of OpenFaaS is simple. It consists of the API gateway for accepting requests. The API gateway then passes the requests to containers, functions with *watchdogs*, inside the cluster. Watchdog is a component of OpenFaaS which will be discussed shortly, in the next section. The gateway also keeps track of the number of function invocations. When the volume of requests is going to be large, the gateway will trigger the orchestration engine to scale replicas of functions on demand.

- **Open and extensible platform**: OpenFaaS is designed to be open and extensible. With this openness and extensibility, the number of FaaS backends supported by OpenFaaS has been increasing over time, as anyone can contribute a new backend for OpenFaaS. For example, if we want to run functions directly in a container runtime, such as containers, for performance reasons, we can extend OpenFaaS by writing a new containerd backend for it.

- **Language agnostic**: We can write OpenFaaS functions in any language supported by Linux or Windows, then pack them as Docker or OCI container images.

Architecture

We used to build our systems in the **monolithic** style. Now we use microservices. A microservice is definitely decomposable into smaller functions. Obviously, a function is the next step in architectural evolution.

Monolithic is a software architecture that contains distinguishable software concerns. Every service is built into a single deployment module.

The microservice architecture, in contrast, separates coherent services inside a single monolithic module to be externally, loosely coupled services.

Function as a Service or **FaaS** is another level of separation. In this architecture, a microservice is split into more fine-grained units, *functions*:

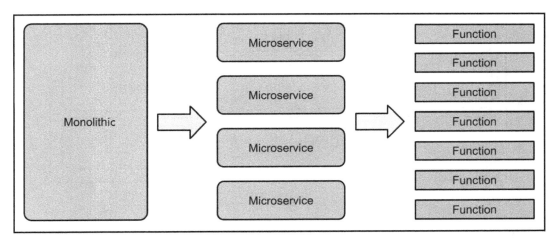

Figure 4.1: Monolithic, microservice, and function architectures

OpenFaaS components

This section explains the components of OpenFaaS. The components are the API gateway, the function watchdog, and an instance of Prometheus. All are running on top of Docker Swarm or Kubernetes orchestration engines. The API gateway and the instance of Prometheus run as services, while the function watchdog runs as the part of function containers. The container runtime can be any modern version of Docker or containerd:

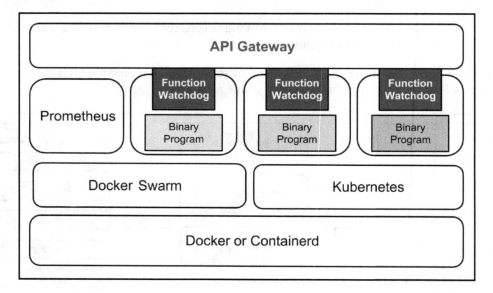

Figure 4.2: An overview of the OpenFaaS architecture

The client could be `curl`, `faas-cli`, or any HTTP-based client that is able to connect to the API gateway in order to invoke a function. A function container, having a function watchdog as its sidecar (an implementation pattern that lets another sidecar process run alongside the main process in the same container), lives in the cluster behind the API gateway. Each service is communicating via the main overlay network, `func_functions` by default:

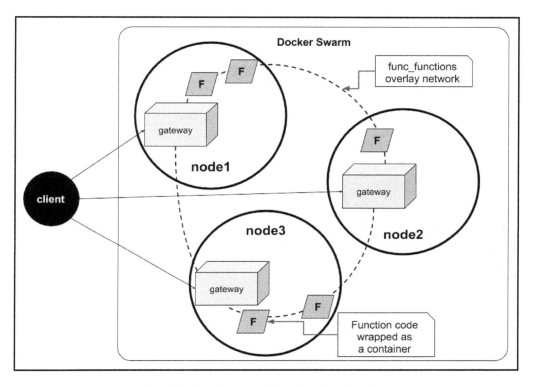

Figure 4.3: The internal infrastructure of OpenFaaS running on Docker Swarm

Function watchdog

The function watchdog is an OpenFaaS component. It is responsible for wrapping the real working code around a function program. The function program's requirement is only to accept input via the **standard input** (**stdin**) and print out the result, of course, to the **standard output** (**stdout**).

The API gateway (`gateway`) connects to function containers through an overlay network. Each function container contains the following:

- Function watchdog, `fwatchdog`
- A certain function program written in any language

The Dockerfile describing a function container must have the `fprocess` environment variable pointing to the function program name and arguments:

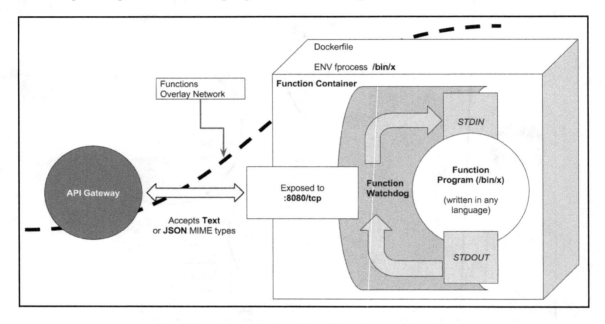

Figure 4.4: Interaction between function watchdog and the function program in the container

Command-line interface

The OpenFaaS command-line interface is just another way to use OpenFaaS. The latest version of the CLI can be obtained directly from the installation script at `https://cli.openfaas.com`. For both Linux and macOS, the CLI can be installed using the following command:

```
$ curl -sL https://cli.openfaas.com | sudo sh
```

Currently, the installation script supports macOS and Linux running on ARM, ARM64, and x64 chips. The CLI has been designed to manage the life cycle of OpenFaaS functions. We can build, deploy, and invoke functions using sub-commands provided by the CLI.

The CLI actually controls OpenFaaS via a set of control plane APIs exposed by its API gateway.

API gateway

The OpenFaaS API gateway provides routing mechanisms to expose your functions to the external world.

When a function is invoked by an external request, the function metric will be collected and put into a Prometheus instance. The API gateway keeps monitoring a number of requests for each function, and scales it on demand by increasing the service replica via the Docker Swarm API. Basically, OpenFaaS fully utilizes the scheduling mechanism of Docker Swarm for its autoscaling. The API gateway also comes with a built-in user interface, called the **UI portal**. The UI allows us to define and invoke functions with a browser.

Installing OpenFaaS

It is extremely simple to install OpenFaaS locally on a development machine. Make sure you have Docker 17.05 or later installed and you will be ready to go.

First, we need to initialize a Swarm cluster. A single node Swarm is enough to be used in the development environment:

```
$ docker swarm init
```

If the Swarm cannot be initialized because the machine has *multiple network interfaces*, we have to specify an IP address or an interface name for the argument, `--advertise-addr`.

OpenFaaS can be up and running directly from its source by cloning the repository from GitHub. Then, check out the OpenFaaS version you want and run the `deploy_stack.sh` script. The following example is to start version 0.6.5 of OpenFaaS. Please note that there is `docker-compose.yml` in this directory, which will be used by the `docker_stack.sh` to deploy the OpenFaaS Docker stack:

```
$ git clone https://github.com/openfaas/faas \
  cd faas \
  git checkout 0.6.5 \
  ./deploy_stack.sh
Cloning into 'faas'...
remote: Counting objects: 11513, done.
remote: Compressing objects: 100% (21/21), done.
remote: Total 11513 (delta 16), reused 19 (delta 8), pack-reused 11484
Receiving objects: 100% (11513/11513), 16.64 MiB | 938.00 KiB/s, done.
Resolving deltas: 100% (3303/3303), done.
```

```
Note: checking out '0.6.5'.
HEAD is now at 5a58db2...

Deploying stack
Creating network func_functions
Creating service func_gateway
Creating service func_alertmanager
Creating service func_echoit
Creating service func_nodeinfo
Creating service func_wordcount
Creating service func_webhookstash
Creating service func_decodebase64
Creating service func_markdown
Creating service func_base64
Creating service func_hubstats
Creating service func_prometheus
```

We now see that a number of services are deployed to the Docker Swarm cluster. It is actually done by running `docker stack deploy` behind the scenes inside the bash script. The Docker stack's name used by OpenFaaS is `func`.

To check whether services are deployed properly in the `func` stack, we use `docker stack ls` to list stacks and their running services:

```
$ docker stack ls
NAME    SERVICES
func    11
```

Now we know that there is a stack of 11 services named `func`. Let's check their details with `docker stack services func`. We use the format argument to let the `docker stack services func` command show each service's name and port. You can leave out the `--format` to see all information about each service:

```
$ docker stack services func --format "table {{.Name}}\t{{.Ports}}"
NAME                    PORTS
func_hubstats
func_markdown
func_echoit
func_webhookstash
func_prometheus         *:9090->9090/tcp
func_gateway            *:8080->8080/tcp
func_decodebase64
func_base64
func_wordcount
func_alertmanager       *:9093->9093/tcp
func_nodeinfo
```

After everything is up and running, the OpenFaaS portal can be opened via
`http://127.0.0.1:8080`. The following screenshot shows the browser running
OpenFaaS Portal. All available functions are listed in the left panel. When clicking a
function name, the main panel will show the function's details. We can play around with
each function by clicking the **INVOKE** button on the main panel:

Figure 4.5: The OpenFaaS UI invoking an example function

We will learn how to prepare a function to run on the OpenFaaS platform in the next
section.

Preparing a function

Before a function can be deployed and invoked, we need to prepare a binary program and
pack it as a function container.

Here are the steps to package your program into a function container:

1. Create a Dockerfile containing the FROM instruction to derive it from a base image. You can even use the Alpine base image.
2. Add the function watchdog binary to the image using the ADD instruction. The function watchdog's name is fwatchdog and can be found on the OpenFaaS release page.
3. Add the function program to the image. We usually use the COPY instruction to do so.
4. Define the environment variable named fprocess with the ENV instruction to point to our function program.
5. Expose port 8080 for this container image using the EXPOSE instruction with, of course, port number 8080.
6. Define an entry point of this container image. We use ENTRYPOINT to point to fwatchdog.

We will do something a bit unusual, but in the proper way, to prepare a function container. We use a Docker feature called **multi-stage builds** to both compile the program and pack the function container using a single Dockerfile.

 What is multi-stage build? The multi-stage build feature allows a single Dockerfile to have several build stages chaining along the build process.

With this technique, we can build a very tiny Docker image by discarding large image layers from the previous build stages. This feature requires Docker 17.05 or greater.

Packing a C program

Here's an unusual, but simple, example of a function. In this example, we'll try to compile, pack, and deploy a C program as a function. Why a C program? Basically, if we know that we can pack a C program, then any traditional program could be compiled and packed in a similar way.

We know that when we design a function, it receives an input from stdin and sends an output to stdout. A C program will then send a simple sentence out to stdout, of course with printf():

```
#include <stdio.h>

int main() {
  printf("%s\n", "hello function");
  return 0;
}
```

Normally, this C program can be compiled using gcc before copying and packing it as a container. But to make a Dockerfile self-contained, the multi-stage build technique will be used to compile and pack it as a function using a single docker build command.

The following multi-stage Dockerfile consists of two stages. State 0 starts with the Alpine 3.6 image, then installs gcc and musl-dev for compiling a C program. There is a command to build the C program statically, gcc -static, so that it does not require any shared object libraries:

```
###############
# State 0
###############
FROM alpine:3.6

RUN apk update apk add gcc musl-dev

COPY main.c /root/
WORKDIR /root/

RUN gcc -static -o main main.c

###############
# State 1
###############
FROM alpine:3.6
ADD https://github.com/openfaas/faas/releases/download/0.6.5/fwatchdog
/usr/bin/

RUN chmod +x /usr/bin/fwatchdog
EXPOSE 8080

COPY --from=0 /root/main /usr/bin/func_c
ENV fprocess="/usr/bin/func_c"

ENTRYPOINT ["/usr/bin/fwatchdog"]
```

Stage 1 also starts with the Alpine 3.6 base image. It adds the `fwatchdog` binary directly from the OpenFaaS GitHub release page and changes its mode to be executable (`chmod +x`). The most important part of this Dockerfile is when it copies the main binary from the previous state, **Stage 0**. This can be done using the `COPY` instruction with the `--from` argument. The build process of the `func_c` container image is illustrated here:

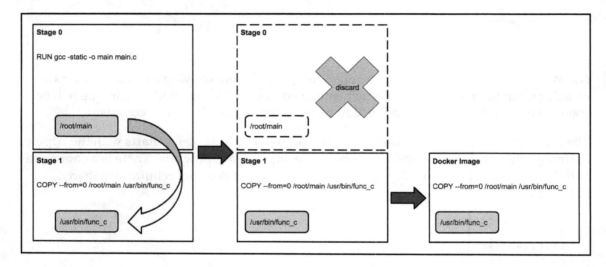

Figure 4.6: Illustration of multi-stage build workflow from the example

The following line from the previous Dockerfile shows how to use the `COPY` instruction to copy a file between stages. In **Stage 1**, the `COPY --from=0` means that the command will copy a file or a set of files from **Stage 0** to **Stage 1**. In the previous example, it will change the `/root/main` file from **Stage 0** to be `/usr/bin/func_c` in **Stage 1**:

```
COPY --from=0 /root/main /usr/bin/func_c
```

As the multi-stage Dockerfile is ready, the next step is to `docker build` with that Dockerfile.

Before doing this, an environment variable, `DOCKER_ID`, will be set to be your Docker ID. If you do not have one, please visit `https://hub.docker.com` and sign up there. The use of this `DOCKER_ID` variable will allow you to follow the commands without changing my Docker ID to yours for every code snippet:

```
$ export DOCKER_ID="chanwit"           # replace this to yours Docker ID.
$ docker build -t $DOCKER_ID/func_c .  # <- please note that there's a dot
here.
```

The running state of the function container will look like the image stack illustrated in *Figure 4.7*. The lowest level is the root filesystem on top of the operating system's kernel. The next levels are the base image and the image layers mounted on top of each other, using the capability of a union filesystem. The top-most layer is a writable file system for each running container that represents an OpenFaaS function:

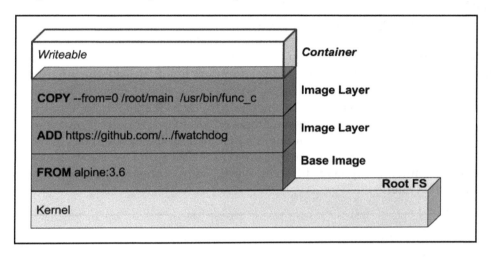

Figure 4.7: A function as a running container with a writable file system layer on top

With multi-stage builds, we can create a very small image containing only the binary files needed to be a function. By discarding the whole of **Stage 0**'s image layers, consisting of all compiler and dependency stuff, the final image size is reduced to be just around 11 MB in total. It can be checked by running `docker image ls $DOCKER_ID/func_c`:

```
$ docker image ls $DOCKER_ID/func_c
REPOSITORY        TAG      IMAGE ID        CREATED          SIZE
chanwit/func_c    latest   b673f7f37036    35 minutes ago   11.6MB
```

Please note that the OpenFaaS mechanism will look for an image from the repository first. So, before using the container image as a function, it would be safe to push the image to Docker Hub, or your repository. This can simply be done using the `docker image push` command. Please note that you may require `docker login` to authenticate with Docker Hub before pushing the image:

```
$ docker image push $DOCKER_ID/func_c
```

Defining and invoking a function with the UI

It is really simple to define and invoke a function on OpenFaaS. After pushing the image, a function can be defined via the OpenFaaS UI Portal. First, open `http://127.0.0.1:8080/ui`. Then, you will see a clickable label, **CREATE NEW FUNCTION**, in the left panel. After clicking it, dialog for defining a function will pop up. It requires the Docker image name for this function; in this case, the image name will be `chanwit/func_c`. Again, please do not forget to change my Docker ID to yours. Second, the definition requires a function name. Just name it `func_c`. Third, we need to define the value for the `fprocess` field pointing to the command line to invoke the binary program. In this example, the command line will simply be `/usr/bin/func_c` inside the container. If the function program requires some parameters, also include them there. Finally, the function definition requires the name of a Docker overlay network to allow the API gateway to connect to the function containers. Just include the default one, `func_functions`, there. It is really important to note that if an OpenFaaS stack is deployed to another environment, and has a different overlay network name, you must not forget to specify the correct one:

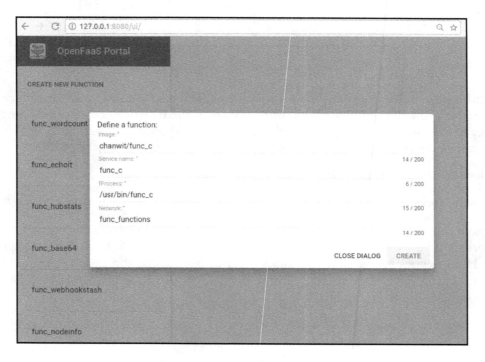

Figure 4.8: Defining an OpenFaaS function via the UI

If everything looks fine, click **CREATE** to define the function. After creation, the func_c function will be listed in the left panel. Clicking on the function's name will show the main panel for function invocation, as follows:

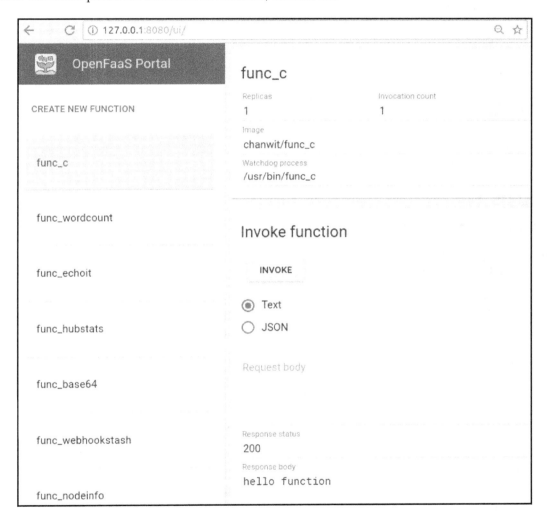

Figure 4.9: Invocation of the func_c function with its response body

If a function requires any input, the input data in the form of text or JSON can be placed as the **Request body**. However, the `func_c` function does not accept any input, so just press the **INVOKE** button and the function will be called. In the example, the invocation process is completed and its status is OK: `200`. The API gateway gets the STDOUT from the function's binary, `/usr/bin/func_c`, and shows it here as the **Response body** in text format.

Using the OpenFaaS CLI

The OpenFaaS CLI, `faas-cli`, is a command-line tool to help manage, prepare, and invoke functions. On Linux, the OpenFaaS CLI can be installed using the following command:

```
$ curl -sSL https://cli.openfaas.com | sudo sh
```

On macOS, it can be installed via `brew` with the following command:

```
$ brew install faas-cli
```

Alternatively, on Windows, `faas-cli.exe` can be downloaded directly from the OpenFaaS GitHub repository and run manually.

However, we assume that every example is running on Linux. In the following example, the `hello` function will be created using OpenFaaS's template for the Go language, which can be found at `openfaas/fass-cli` in GitHub in the `template/go` directory.

Locally, all templates will be stored in the `template/` directory of the working directory. If the template directory does not exist, all templates will be fetched from GitHub's, `openfaas/faas-cli`. As of OpenFaaS 0.6, there are 10 available templates for five different programming languages there.

Defining a new function

To create a function written in the Go language, we use the `faas-cli new --lang=go hello` command:

```
$ faas-cli new --lang=go hello

2017/11/15 18:42:28 No templates found in current directory.
2017/11/15 18:42:28 HTTP GET
https://github.com/openfaas/faas-cli/archive/master.zip
2017/11/15 18:42:38 Writing 287Kb to master.zip
```

```
2017/11/15 18:42:38 Attempting to expand templates from master.zip
2017/11/15 18:42:38 Fetched 10 template(s) : [csharp go-armhf go node-arm64
node-armhf node python-armhf python python3 ruby] from
https://github.com/openfaas/faas-cli
2017/11/15 18:42:38 Cleaning up zip file...
Folder: hello created.
```

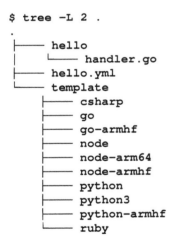

```
Function created in folder: hello
Stack file written: hello.yml
```

After the function is created, we can check the structure of the function directory by running the tree -L 2 . command. It shows the directory at two levels of depth, as follows:

```
$ tree -L 2 .
.
├── hello
│   └── handler.go
├── hello.yml
└── template
    ├── csharp
    ├── go
    ├── go-armhf
    ├── node
    ├── node-arm64
    ├── node-armhf
    ├── python
    ├── python3
    ├── python-armhf
    └── ruby
```

First, we will look at the function definition in the hello.yml file. From hello.yml, there are two top-levels, provider and functions.

The provider block tells us that its provider's name is faas, the default OpenFaaS implementation in Docker Swarm. Also, it tells us that the gateway endpoint is at http://localhost:8080, where an instance of the API gateway is running. In a production environment, this URL could be changed to point to the real IP address.

The `functions` block lists all defined functions. In the example, there is only the `hello` function there. This block tells us this function is written in the Go programming language (`lang: go`). The function's handler specified by `handler: ./hello` points to the directory containing the source file of the real working function (`./hello/handler.go`). In the example, the output image's name is specified by `image: hello`. Before building the function, we would change the image name to `<your Docker ID>/hello:v1` as it is a best practice to not use the `:latest` tag:

```
############
# hello.yml
############
provider:
  name: faas
  gateway: http://localhost:8080

functions:
  hello:
    lang: go
    handler: ./hello
    image: hello  # change this line to <your Docker ID>/hello:v1
```

Building and pushing

We will edit the last line to be `image: chanwit/hello:v1`. Again, do not forget to replace my Docker ID with yours. We then build with the `faas-cli build` command. We use `-f` to specify a function definition file for the CLI. Please note that there will be two stages and 17 steps to build this Dockerfile:

```
$ faas-cli build -f ./hello.yml
[0] > Building: hello.
Clearing temporary build folder: ./build/hello/
Preparing ./hello/ ./build/hello/function
Building: chanwit/hello:v1 with go template. Please wait..

Sending build context to Docker daemon  6.144kB
Step 1/17 : FROM golang:1.8.3-alpine3.6
 ---> fd1ada53b403

. . .

Step 17/17 : CMD ./fwatchdog
 ---> Running in a904f6659c33
 ---> f3b8ec154ee9
Removing intermediate container a904f6659c33
```

```
Successfully built f3b8ec154ee9
Successfully tagged chanwit/hello:v1
Image: chanwit/hello:v1 built.
[0] < Builder done.
```

The Go function template will be copied from the `template/go` directory to the `build/hello` directory. Then the handler file, `hello/handler.go`, will be copied to `build/hello/function/handler.go`. The program's entry point is defined in `build/hello/main.go`, which in turn calls the handler function. During the build process, the `docker build` command will be executed internally by `faas-cli`. Steps defined inside the Dockerfile will be used to compile and pack the function.

The following figure explains how the Dockerfile, the source files, and the template are related to each other:

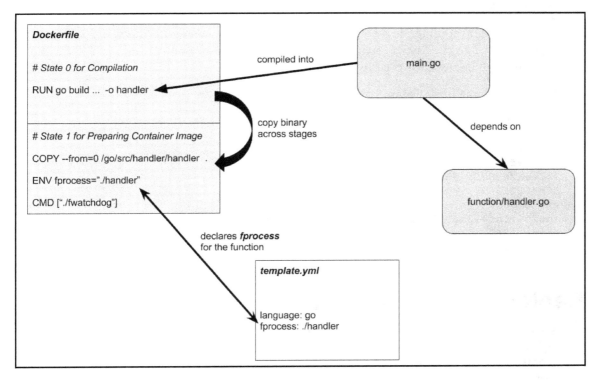

Figure 4.10: OpenFaaS template and its related components for the Go language

After the build is completed, we check the directory's structure again. This time, run `tree -L 3 .` to show the directory for three levels of depth because we want to inspect the contents of the `build` directory, which is created by the `faas-cli build` command:

```
$ tree -L 3 .
.
├── build
│   └── hello
│       ├── Dockerfile
│       ├── function
│       ├── main.go
│       └── template.yml
├── hello
│   └── handler.go
├── hello.yml
└── template
```

We can push the built image to a Docker repository directly, also with the `faas-cli push` command. Use `-f` to specify the specification file. The value of `functions.image` for the specification will be used for pushing:

```
$ faas-cli push -f hello.yml
[0] > Pushing: hello.
The push refers to a repository [docker.io/chanwit/hello]
8170484ad942: Pushed
071849fe2878: Pushed
a2e6c9f93e16: Pushed
76eeaa2cc808: Pushed
3fb66f713c9f: Pushed
v1: digest:
sha256:fbf493a6bb36ef92f14578508f345f055f346d0aecc431aa3f84a4f0db04e7cb
size: 1367
[0] < Pushing done.
```

Deploying and invoking

To deploy the newly built function, we use the `faas-cli deploy` command. It reads the function specification with `-f`, similar to other sub-commands. In this example, it uses the value of the provider's gateway to deploy the function. If there's already a previous function running as a service on Docker Swarm, the old one will be deleted before deploying the new one. After deployment, the URL for manually invoking the function, such as via `curl`, will be shown:

```
$ faas-cli deploy -f hello.yml
```

```
Deploying: hello.
Removing old function.
Deployed.
URL: http://localhost:8080/function/hello

200 OK
```

To obtain all running functions on the cluster, we can run the `faas-cli list` command. The command also shows the number of invocations done on each function, and the number of replicas for function instances. The replicas will be increased automatically when the invocation rate gets high enough. All of this information is stored inside the instance of Prometheus. We will see it in a better way, with a Grafana dashboard, in the next section:

```
$ faas-cli list
Function                    Invocations        Replicas
func_echoit                 0                  1
func_wordcount              0                  1
func_webhookstash           0                  1
func_markdown               0                  1
func_hubstats               0                  1
func_decodebase64           0                  1
hello                       0                  1
func_base64                 0                  1
func_nodeinfo               0                  1
```

The `hello` function accepts input via `stdin` and output via `stdout`. To test invocation of the function, a sentence is echoed and piped to the `stdin` of the command `faas-cli invoke`. This invocation is processed via the OpenFaaS framework, and all invocation stats are recorded on a Prometheus instance in the cluster:

```
$ echo "How are you?" | faas-cli invoke hello
Hello, Go. You said: How are you?
```

Templates

The predefined templates may be good enough for strings and developing simple functions, but when things get complex, it is great to know how to tweak OpenFaaS templates by ourselves.

In this section, the Go template will be tweaked to simply reduce the number of build steps as an example. The following Dockerfile of the Go template can be found at `template/go/Dockerfile`. This Dockerfile already uses the multi-stage build technique:

```
###################
# State 0
###################
FROM golang:1.8.3-alpine3.6

# ... lines removed for brevity

###################
# State 1
###################
FROM alpine:3.6
RUN apk --no-cache add ca-certificates

# Add non root user
RUN addgroup -S app adduser -S -g app app \
    mkdir -p /home/app \
    chown app /home/app

WORKDIR /home/app
COPY --from=0 /go/src/handler/handler    .
COPY --from=0 /usr/bin/fwatchdog         .

USER app
ENV fprocess="./handler"
CMD ["./fwatchdog"]
```

Templates can be hosted on a custom Git repository. Here's the structure of a template repository, which can be fetched by the `template` sub-command. The first level must be a directory named `template/`. Inside the `template` directory, there may be a number of directories, for example, `go/` in the following structure:

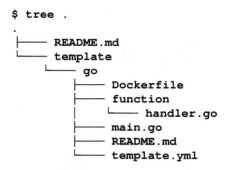

```
$ tree .
.
├── README.md
└── template
    └── go
        ├── Dockerfile
        ├── function
        │   └── handler.go
        ├── main.go
        ├── README.md
        └── template.yml
```

After storing the whole template source in a GitHub repository, it can be pulled for building and tweaking later with `faas-cli template pull`:

```
$ faas-cli template pull https://github.com/chanwit/faas-templates
Fetch templates from repository: https://github.com/chanwit/faas-templates
2017/11/16 15:44:46 HTTP GET
https://github.com/chanwit/faas-templates/archive/master.zip
2017/11/16 15:44:48 Writing 2Kb to master.zip

2017/11/16 15:44:48 Attempting to expand templates from master.zip
2017/11/16 15:44:48 Fetched 1 template(s) : [go] from
https://github.com/chanwit/faas-templates
2017/11/16 15:44:48 Cleaning up zip file...
```

After pulling the tweaked template, the image can be rebuilt and the number of build steps is reduced to *15*:

```
$ faas-cli build -f hello.yml
[0] > Building: hello.
Clearing temporary build folder: ./build/hello/
Preparing ./hello/ ./build/hello/function
Building: chanwit/hello:v1 with go template. Please wait..
Sending build context to Docker daemon    7.68kB
Step 1/15 : FROM golang:1.8.3-alpine3.6
 ---> fd1ada53b403

...

Step 15/15 : CMD ./fwatchdog
 ---> Using cache
 ---> 23dfcc80a031
Successfully built 23dfcc80a031
Successfully tagged chanwit/hello:v1
Image: chanwit/hello:v1 built.
[0] < Builder done.
```

The OpenFaaS dashboard

A good OpenFaaS dashboard is available on the Grafana platform. To make Grafana work with OpenFaaS, the Grafana server must be on the same network. We can use the following command to run a Grafana server via `docker service create` outside the OpenFaaS stack. It links to the OpenFaaS stack via the `--network=func_functions` argument:

```
$ docker service create --name=grafana \
    --network=func_functions \
    -p 3000:3000 grafana/grafana
```

Alternatively, open the dashboard at `http://localhost:3000`. Log in using the username `admin` and password `admin`:

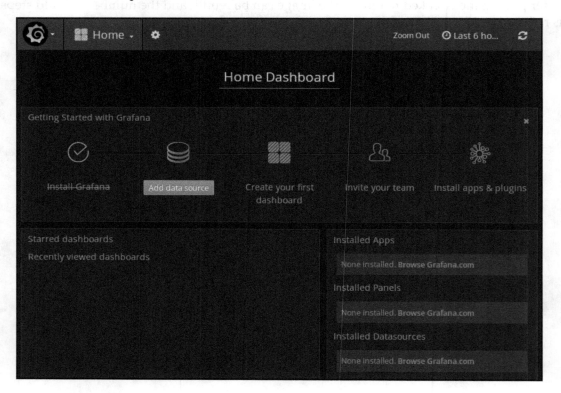

Figure 4.11: Grafana home dashboard

A data source has to be created and pointed to the Prometheus server before using it as the source of a dashboard. Firstly, the data source name must be `prometheus`. Secondly, the URL needs to point to `http://prometheus:9090`. After that, we can click the **Save** and **Test** buttons. A green popup will be displayed if the data source setting is correct:

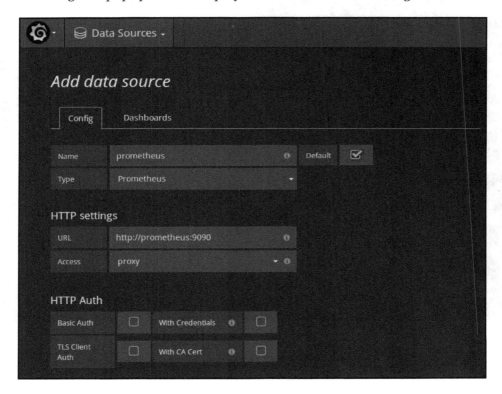

Figure 4.12: Defining a new Prometheus data source in Grafana

Next, an OpenFaaS dashboard can be imported using the dashboard's ID. We will use dashboard number 3434, then click on **Load** to prepare to import the dashboard:

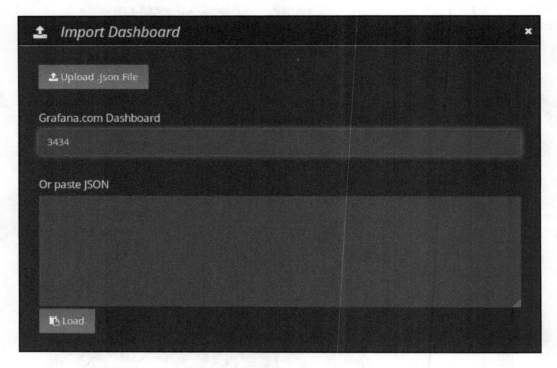

Figure 4.13: The dashboard importing screen in Grafana

Next, the dialog will be changed to **Importing Dashboard from Grafana.com**. Here, it will ask us to include the dashboard name. We can leave it as the default name. It will also ask which data source we would like to use. Choose the Prometheus data source, which s already defined in the previous steps. After that, click the **Import** button to finish the importing process:

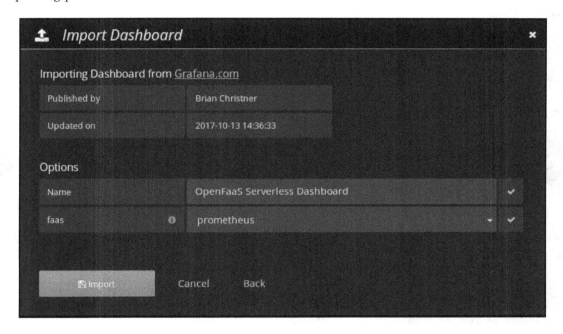

Figure 4.14: Setting the dashboard's name and selecting the Prometheus data source for it

Here's what the dashboard looks like. It displays the gateway's health status in a box and the number of gateway services as a gauge. The total function invocation stat is displayed as a line chart with numbers. The `hello` function written in Go is linearly invoked more than 20,000 times. During the test, the number of function replicas is scaled up, from five to 20. However, it is tested on a single machine, so the invocation rate does not change significantly:

Figure 4.15: The OpenFaaS dashboard in action

Here's the mechanism to allow OpenFaaS to auto-scale function replicas. First, when a client requests function invocation through the API gateway, the invocation will be stored in Prometheus. Inside Prometheus, there is an **Alert Manager**, which is responsible for firing events when a predefined rule is matched. OpenFaaS defines a rule for the **Alert Manager** to scale the number of replicas up by hooking the event with its **Alert Handler** URL, `http://gateway:8080/system/alert`. This **Alert Handler** will take care of calculating the number of replicas, checking the max replicas limit, and scaling the replicas of a certain function by sending the `scale` command to the cluster via the Swarm client API. The following diagram illustrates the steps behind this autoscaling mechanism:

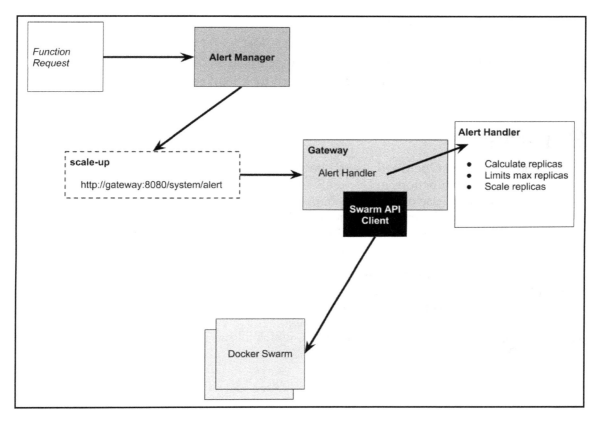

Figure 4.16: The alerting mechanism of OpenFaaS to auto-scale the replicas of function services in the Docker Swarm

Exercises

Here's a list of questions to you help review all of the topics you should remember and understand from this chapter:

1. What are the advantages of using OpenFaaS?
2. Please describe the OpenFaaS architecture. How does each component talk to another?
3. How do we deploy an OpenFaaS stack on the Docker Swarm?
4. Why does OpenFaaS use a multi-stage build?
5. How do we create a new OpenFaaS function for Node.js?
6. How do we build and pack an OpenFaaS function?

7. What is the default name of the overlay network used by OpenFaaS?
8. What is the function template? What is it for?
9. Describe the steps to prepare a custom template and host it on GitHub.
10. How do we define a Grafana dashboard for OpenFaaS?

Summary

This chapter discussed OpenFaaS, its architecture, and how we can use it as a serverless framework to deploy functions in Docker Swarm. OpenFaaS has several compelling features, especially its ease of use. This chapter showed that deploying an OpenFaaS stack is quite simple in Docker Swarm infrastructure. Then, this chapter continued to discuss how to define, build, pack, and deploy functions in OpenFaaS. It also discussed an advanced topic of how to tweak and prepare custom templates.

Monitoring OpenFaaS is quite simple, as it comes with Prometheus built in. We only need to install a Grafana dashboard and connect it to the Prometheus data source and we will have a ready-to-use dashboard, helping us to operate an OpenFaaS cluster.

The next chapter will introduce the Fn Project, which allows us to deploy an FaaS platform on a plain Docker infrastructure.

5
The Fn Project

This chapter introduces an FaaS platform, *the Fn Project*. It is another great FaaS framework developed by a team at Oracle Inc. Fn is one of the easiest projects that allows us to deploy an FaaS platform on a plain Docker infrastructure.

This chapter begins with a discussion of what the Fn Project is. It then moves on to look at how its components are organized and what its overall architecture is. We will then learn how to use the Fn CLI to prepare and deploy functions. The chapter then ends with a discussion of how to use Fn subprojects for its UI, scaling, and monitoring of the Fn cluster itself.

We will cover the following topics in this chapter:

- The Fn Project
- The Fn's architecture
- Using Fn CLI
- Deploying a local function
- Deploying Fn on Docker Swarm
- Monitoring Fn with its built-in UI
- Log analysis with a familiar tool

The Fn Project

The Fn Project was originally devised by the team at *Iron.io* (`https://www.iron.io/`) under the name of Iron function. After that, the two founders joined Oracle and forked Iron function into the new project, Fn.

Fn is a framework and system designed to develop and deploy serverless/FaaS applications. In contrast to OpenFaaS, Fn does not use any of the orchestrator-level features to manage function containers.

Fn does not only support deployment via its own infrastructure; it also allows you to deploy the same functions to AWS Lambda. However, we will scope only for deploying functions to its own infrastructure, which is, of course, Docker-based.

There are several design reasons behind Fn.

The Fn Project is committed to be open source. It natively supports Docker, which means that we could use a Docker container as its deployment unit—**a function**. Fn supports development in any programming language. The Fn infrastructure is written in the Go programming language and aims to be able to deploy everywhere, including the public cloud, a private cloud, and even the hybrid infrastructure. Fn allows for the importing of the Lambda functions from AWS and then deploying them to its own infrastructure.

As previously mentioned, the serverless/FaaS infrastructure with Docker is basically designed to effect a balance between controlling the whole system and the ease of maintenance and administration of the infrastructure. Fn also has the design goals that align with this concept too.

Fn's architecture

The easiest setup of an Fn Server is just bringing up a standalone Fn container; however, the more complete architecture will be as shown here. A cluster implementation will be demonstrated at the end of this chapter. The following diagram shows the overview of the Fn architecture:

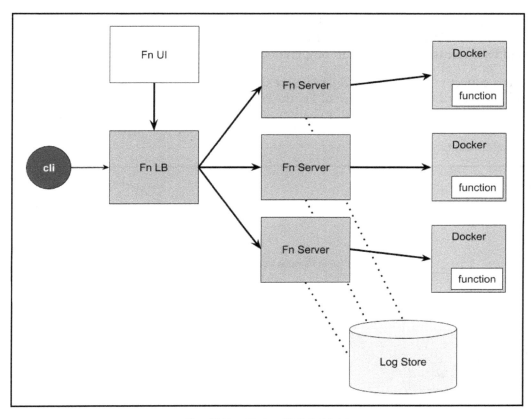

Figure 5.1: The architecture of the Fn FaaS cluster

As is the case with the common FaaS architecture, Fn also has the *API gateway*, which is **Fn LB** in the previous diagram. Fn LB is basically a load balancer. It passes through requests from the client to each **Fn Server**. In the Fn Server implementation, there is no separation concept of *initiator* and *executor* as there is no event bus at the core of the Fn's architecture. So, an Fn Server also acts as an executor to execute functions on its associate Docker engine.

Fn Servers connect to a **Log Store**, which could be a standalone or a cluster of DBMS. All data sent from an Fn function to the standard error is logged to the **Log Store**.

Fn UI and **Fn LB** are extra components to help make the Fn Project better in terms of production. The Fn UI is the user interface server, such as dashboard, for Fn, while Fn LB is the load balancer to round robin among Fn nodes in the cluster.

There is a concept of an *Executor Agent* inside the Fn Server. The agent is responsible for controlling the runtime. In the case of Fn, the runtime is Docker. So, the executor agent is also referred as a *Docker agent* in this chapter. With the default configuration, the Docker agent inside an Fn Server connects to the local Docker engine and starts Fn functions via a local Unix socket:

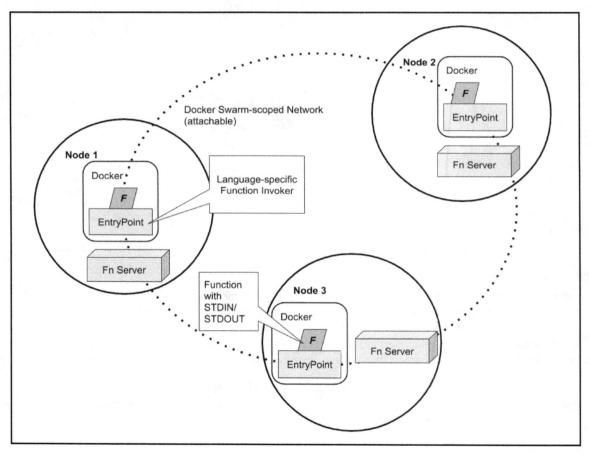

Figure 5.2: A diagram showing an Fn cluster over a Swarm-scoped network

The previous diagram shows a running Fn cluster over a Swarm-scoped overlay network. To form a cluster, we will use an attachable Swarm-scoped network. Each Fn Server instance has to attach to the network. When a request is made to the gateway or directly to the server, it will be passed through to the **EntryPoint**. The EntryPoint is a language-specific program that wraps around the real function program. For example, in the case of an Fn function built with Java, the EntryPoint is the class `com.fnproject.fn.runtime.EntryPoint`. There is a code inside this Java class to invoke the real function via Java's reflection technique:

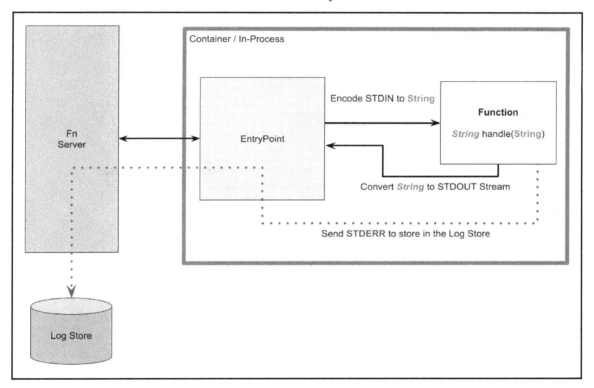

Figure 5.3: An Fn function interacting with STDIN, STDOUT, and writing logs to STDERR, where it delegates logs to the store

The Fn Server sends the request body in the form of **STDIN** to the **Function** container. After the **EntryPoint** receives the **STDIN** stream, it converts the data content to match the type of function signature. In the previous diagram, the signature is **String**. So the function body is converted to a string. Output sent to **STDOUT** will be forwarded to the **Fn Server** and sent out as the result, while output sent to **STDERR** will be captured and stored in the **Log Store**.

Using Fn CLI

This section will discuss how to use the basics of the Fn CLI, a command line to control Fn. Let's start with the installation of the Fn CLI. Make sure that the `curl` command exists on your system:

```
$ curl -LSs https://raw.githubusercontent.com/fnproject/cli/master/install
| sh
```

After installing the previous command, check its version and help by typing `fn`. The current version of the command line is `0.4.43` at the time of writing. Things move fast, so you can expect to use the different version anyway:

```
$ fn
fn 0.4.43

Fn command line tool

ENVIRONMENT VARIABLES:
    FN_API_URL - Fn server address
    FN_REGISTRY - Docker registry to push images to, use username only to
push to Docker Hub - [[registry.hub.docker.com/]USERNAME]

COMMANDS:
    ...
```

There are several sub-commands provided by `fn`, for example:

- `fn start` is a thin wrapper around the `docker run` command. This subcommand starts the new Fn Server instance. The default address will be `http://localhost:8080`. The Fn CLI will however be trying to connect to the address defined in `FN_API_URL`, if set as an environment variable.
- `fn update` is the command for pulling the latest version of the Fn Server to a local Docker image.
- `fn init` is the command for initializing a skeleton to develop a new function. It accepts the `--runtime` parameter to generate the template for a specific language, such as Go, for example.
- `fn apps` contains subcommands for creating, updating, and deleting an application, and is a kind of namespace or package to group functions together. It is required that a function must be defined under an application.

- `fn routes` is a set of commands to define a route pointing to a function container. For example, we have the application `demo`, then we can define the route, `hello` and point it to the Docker container image, `test/hello:v1`. An application may be many routes:

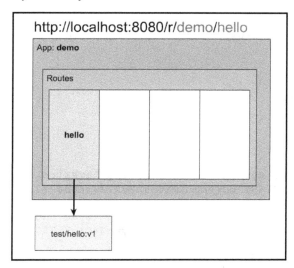

Figure 5.4: The relation between an Fn application and its routes

Here's how Fn organizes routes under an application. For example, an Fn's API URL is `http://localhost:8080`. We may have an application named `demo` containing a route named `hello` created for the container image, `test/hello:v1`. All these together form a fully qualified URL for accessing the function.

Let's deploy a local function

Firstly, carry out `fn start` to up a standalone Fn Server instance. The server is started by setting up the log level to be `info`, the default setting. The Fn Server then connects to the datastore, the Log Store. The current implementation is SQLite3. After that, the agent will be started. The Docker agent connects to the local Docker engine with its default configuration. Finally, the Fn starts listening to port `8080`:

```
$ fn start

time="2018-03-17T08:48:39Z" level=info msg="Setting log level to"
level=info
time="2018-03-17T08:48:39Z" level=info msg="datastore dialed"
```

```
datastore=sqlite3 max_idle_connections=256
time="2018-03-17T08:48:40Z" level=info msg="agent starting
cfg=&{MinDockerVersion:17.06.0-ce FreezeIdle:50ms EjectIdle:1s
HotPoll:200ms HotLauncherTimeout:1h0m0s AsyncChewPoll:1m0s
MaxResponseSize:0 MaxLogSize:1048576 MaxTotalCPU:0 MaxTotalMemory:0
MaxFsSize:0}"
time="2018-03-17T08:48:40Z" level=info msg="no docker auths from config
files found (this is fine)" error="open /root/.dockercfg: no such file or
directory"
```

```
time="2018-03-17T08:48:41Z" level=info msg="available memory"
availMemory=12357627495 cgroupLimit=9223372036854771712 headRoom=1373069721
totalMemory=13730697216
time="2018-03-17T08:48:41Z" level=info msg="sync and async ram
reservations" ramAsync=9886101996 ramAsyncHWMark=7908881596
ramSync=2471525499
time="2018-03-17T08:48:41Z" level=info msg="available cpu" availCPU=4000
totalCPU=4000
time="2018-03-17T08:48:41Z" level=info msg="sync and async cpu
reservations" cpuAsync=3200 cpuAsyncHWMark=2560 cpuSync=800
time="2018-03-17T08:48:41Z" level=info msg="Fn serving on `:8080`"
type=full
```

To check whether Docker started the Fn Server properly, we can use `docker ps` to see the running container. This would be done in another Terminal:

```
$ docker ps --format="table {{.ID}}\t{{.Names}}\t{{.Ports}}"
CONTAINER ID     NAMES         PORTS
ab5cd794b787     fnserver      2375/tcp, 0.0.0.0:8080->8080/tcp
```

OK, now we have the Fn Server running on port `8080` as we see the mapping `0.0.0.0:8080->8080/tcp` from `docker ps`.

At the current directory that started the `fn start` command, the container mapped its `data` directory to the host's `$PWD/data`. The directory contains SQLite3 database files to store logs and information. In the production environment, we will replace this with MySQL DBMS, for example:

```
$ tree
.
└── data
    ├── fn.db
    └── fn.mq

1 directory, 2 files
```

To see the list of applications, simply use the `fn apps list` command:

```
$ fn apps list
no apps found
```

Well, there is no newly created application as we have just started the server instance. We will create one. Name it `demo` and use `fn apps list` command again to double-check the created app:

```
$ fn apps create demo
Successfully created app: demo

$ fn apps list
demo
```

Now we will start developing a function. In this example, we use the Java runtime and later on, we will try another runtime for Go.

Let's initialize the new function. We use `fn init` to create a new function project. This command takes `--runtime` to specify a language runtime we would like to use.

The `func.yaml` is our function descriptor. It contains the version number, runtime, and the EntryPoint of the function:

```
$ fn init --runtime java hello
Creating function at: /hello
Runtime: java
Function boilerplate generated.
func.yaml created.
```

We will try to learn how to build and deploy a function. So let's build it without modifying anything first. To build the function, simply use `fn build`. And to deploy the function, we have `fn deploy` to take care of the process for us.

Here's the Fn build behavior. After calling the `fn build` command, the build process starts by using the generated Dockerfile. The resulting image will be tagged and stored locally by the Docker engine. For example, the image in the example will be tagged as `hello:0.0.1` locally. Then, with the `fn deploy` command, it requires `--registry` to store the image remotely on Docker Hub. In this example, my Docker's ID is used. Please do not forget to change it to yours.

The `fn deploy` command works like this.

First, it increases the version number of the function. Second, it pushes the function's image onto Docker Hub using the `--registry` as the repository name. So, `hello:0.0.2` becomes `chanwit/hello:0.0.2` on the Docker Hub.

Then the `fn deploy` will register a new route under the application specified by `--app` using the newly built image's name:

```
$ fn build
Building image hello:0.0.1
Function hello:0.0.1 built successfully.

$ fn deploy --app demo --registry chanwit
Deploying hello to app: demo at path: /hello
Bumped to version 0.0.2
Building image chanwit/hello:0.0.2
Pushing chanwit/hello:0.0.2 to docker registry...The push refers to
repository [docker.io/chanwit/hello]
07a85412c682: Pushed
895a2a3582de: Mounted from fnproject/fn-java-fdk
5fb388f17d37: Mounted from fnproject/fn-java-fdk
c5e4fcfb11b0: Mounted from fnproject/fn-java-fdk
ae882186dfca: Mounted from fnproject/fn-java-fdk
aaf375487746: Mounted from fnproject/fn-java-fdk
51980d95baf3: Mounted from fnproject/fn-java-fdk
0416abcc3238: Mounted from fnproject/fn-java-fdk
0.0.2: digest:
sha256:c7539b1af68659477efac2e180abe84dd79a3de5ccdb9b4d8c59b4c3ea429402
size: 1997
Updating route /hello using image chanwit/hello:0.0.2...
```

Let's check the newly registered route. We use the `fn routes list <app>` command to list all routes under the application `<app>`. In the following example, all routes of `demo` were listed:

```
$ fn routes list demo
path       image                   endpoint
/hello     chanwit/hello:0.0.2     localhost:8080/r/demo/hello
```

The previous command also listed the endpoint of each route. With the endpoint, we could basically use `curl` to interact with it, just like a normal HTTP endpoint. Do not forget to set the `-v` verbose option to `curl`. With this option, we can examine what is hidden inside the HTTP headers.

Let's see the lines marked bold in the HTTP response headers. There are some extra entries, `Fn_call_id` and `Xxx-Fxlb-Wait`.

The header, `Fn_call_id`, is the identifier for each call. This ID will also be used when we enable distributed tracing within Fn. The header, `Xxx-Fxlb-Wait` is the information collectible by the Fn LB, so it knows the wait time of this function:

```
$ curl -v localhost:8080/r/demo/hello

* Trying 127.0.0.1...
* Connected to localhost (127.0.0.1) port 8080 (#0)
> GET /r/demo/hello HTTP/1.1
> Host: localhost:8080
> User-Agent: curl/7.47.0
> Accept: */*
>
< HTTP/1.1 200 OK
< Content-Length: 13
< Content-Type: text/plain
< Fn_call_id: 01C8SPGSEK47WGG00000000000
< Xxx-Fxlb-Wait: 78.21µs
< Date: Sat, 17 Mar 2018 10:01:43 GMT
<
* Connection #0 to host localhost left intact
Hello, world!
```

Trying again with Golang

Let's try creating the next function with another runtime, Go. Unlike Java, Go codes inside an Fn function do not have a proper concept of EntryPoint. Fortunately, the execution model of Fn is simple enough, so this matter is extremely trivial:

```
$ fn init --runtime go hello_go

Creating function at: /hello_go
Runtime: go
Function boilerplate generated.
func.yaml created.
```

Here's the list of files for the Go Fn function:

```
$ cd hello_go

$ tree .
.
├────── func.go
├────── func.yaml
└────── test.json
```

The file, func.go is, of course, the *function program* itself, while func.yaml is the Fn's function *descriptor*. And the one interesting file here is test.json – a file containing test fixtures for functional tests. Currently, we can use the fn test command to test the positive paths, but not the negative results.

We will take a look at func.yaml to see what's inside it first. The version will be automatically increased every time it is deployed. The runtime here is go as we specified it as the --runtime parameter of fn init. The entrypoint here should not be touched. Just leave it there, trust me:

```
$ cat func.yaml

version: 0.0.1
runtime: go
entrypoint: ./func
```

The Go codes could consume the STDIN directly. The best way is to pass the input as a JSON and use Go's `encoding/json` package to process the data. Here's the example adapted from the original Fn example. This program was modified to simplify the output process and add error checking and logging:

```go
package main

import (
  "encoding/json"
  "fmt"
  "os"
)

type Message struct {
  Name string
}

func main() {
  m := &Message{Name: "world"}

  err := json.NewDecoder(os.Stdin).Decode(m)
  if err != nil {
    fmt.Fprintf(os.Stderr, "err JSON Decode: %s\n", err.Error())
    os.Exit(250)
  }

  fmt.Printf(`{"success": "Hello %s"}`, m.Name);
  os.Exit(0)
}
```

In every program, we need to check errors and handle them. As shown in the previous example, we check errors occurring during encoding and then print the error message to `os.Stderr`, the standard error file in Go. Then we just exit the process with code > 0. Here, we use 250.

Let's summarize error handling and logging in Fn. First, write messages to STDERR and they will be stored in the logs. Second, exit the process with an error code, that is, > 0. Fn will then mark the container execution as *error*.

Let's see this in action. Make sure we have the previous code example inside `func.go` and deploy it with the `fn deploy` command:

```
$ fn deploy --app demo --registry chanwit

Deploying hello_go to app: demo at path: /hello_go
Bumped to version 0.0.2
```

```
Building image chanwit/hello_go:0.0.2 .......
Pushing chanwit/hello_go:0.0.2 to docker registry...The push refers to
repository [docker.io/chanwit
/hello_go]
00a6a1467505: Pushed
96252b84ae14: Pushed
97dedccb7128: Mounted from fnproject/go
c9e8b5c053a2: Mounted from fnproject/go
0.0.2: digest:
sha256:8a57737bff7a8e4444921959532716654230af0534b93dc6be247ac88e4e7ef2
size: 1155
Updating route /hello_go using image chanwit/hello_go:0.0.2...
```

If the last line of `fn deploy` is saying that the route is updated, it will be good to go.

Next, we will use the `fn call` command to invoke the function, which is now registered as a route under the app `demo`. Try calling it without parameters to cause the error:

```
$ fn call demo /hello_go

{"error":{"message":"container exit code 250"}}
ERROR: error calling function: status 502
```

This is what we would expect. It was a call without input. So the `encoding/json` raised the error and the program wrote a log message in STDERR (not shown in the previous code). Finally, the function returns `250`. With the message, we saw the `fn call` printed out, saying the function container exited with code `250`. So the error was handled properly.

No log messages here, but we will get back to them later.

Next, we will make a successful call. To make it green, just pass the JSON body using the `echo` command. The JSON body will be piped to `fn call` and turned into a HTTP request, then it will be received by the Fn Server and serialized again to be STDIN for the function program.

The success JSON chuck is what we would expect for a program working correctly.

The syntax of calling a remote function via `fn call` is that we need to pass the *application name* and the *route name* for it to invoke:

```
$ echo '{"Name": "chanwit"}' | fn call demo /hello_go

{"success": "Hello chanwit"}
```

Examining call logs and errors

To see all call logs, use the `fn calls` command. Please note that it's the `calls` command with an *s*. The `fn calls list` command accepts the name of the application. The attributes to focus on are `ID`, and `Status`. The following example shows two call logs, the first one is `error` and the second one is `success`, in reverse chronological order:

```
$ fn calls list demo

ID: 01C8VRGN9R47WGJ00000000000
App: demo
Route: /hello_go
Created At: 2018-03-18T05:15:04.376Z
Started At: 2018-03-18T05:15:04.738Z
Completed At: 2018-03-18T05:15:07.519Z
Status: success

ID: 01C8VRFE3647WGE00000000000
App: demo
Route: /hello_go
Created At: 2018-03-18T05:14:24.230Z
Started At: 2018-03-18T05:14:24.566Z
Completed At: 2018-03-18T05:14:27.375Z
Status: error
```

Now, we pick the second call ID to get the log messages. The command used for retrieving logs is `fn logs get`. It requires the application name and the call ID:

```
$ fn logs get demo 01C8VRFE3647WGE00000000000
err JSON Decode: EOF
```

The previous log message is the one printed out to `os.Stderr` by the Go program.

Deploying Fn on Docker Swarm

In this example, we start an Fn cluster on a Swarm-scoped network.

Starting with deploying a network, we use `weaveworks/net-plugin` as the backbone network for stability reasons. Please note that the network must be attachable and the subnet must be inside the scope of `10.32.0.0/16`. So, `10.32.3.0/24` is just fine here:

```
$ docker network create \
  --driver weaveworks/net-plugin:2.1.3
  --attachable \
  --subnet 10.32.3.0/24 \
  fn_net
```

Then we prepare a volume for the datastore. As this section also wanted to demonstrate a product-grade setup, we use MySQL as the store rather than the default SQLite3. Using MySQL allows us to horizontally scale the number of Fn Servers.

The volume will be created using the `docker volume create` command. If we'd like to set up a MySQL cluster, the setups would be a bit more complex than this, but it will not be covered by this book:

```
$ docker volume create mysql_vol
```

This is the `docker run` command to start an instance of MySQL. We just attach the instance to the network `fn_net` created previously. We specify the network alias here to ensure that the service must be accessible by the name `mysql`. All environment variables are designed to set up a username, password, and the default database, `fn_db`. Do not forget to bind the volume, `mysql_vol`, to `/var/lib/mysql` inside the container. This is designed to enable the data survive to when the container is removed:

```
$ docker run \
    --detach \
    --name mysql \
    --network fn_net \
    --network-alias mysql \
    -e MYSQL_DATABASE=fn_db \
    -e MYSQL_USER=func \
    -e MYSQL_PASSWORD=funcpass \
    -e MYSQL_RANDOM_ROOT_PASSWORD=yes \
    -v mysql_vol:/var/lib/mysql \
    mysql
```

The next step is to start the Fn Servers. This section demonstrates how to start two Fn Servers pointing to the same Log Store (MySQL). Each Fn Server attaches to the `fn_net`. This first instance is named `fn_0`. An Fn Server requires `FN_DB_URL` to point to an external Log Store, which may be PostgreSQL or MySQL. Just put the complete URL as shown in the following command. We also call the container `fn_0` to make it easier to manage.

When having a setting such as this, the Fn Server becomes completely stateless, where all states will be stored externally to the database. So it is now safe to completely remove the Fn Server containers when things go wrong:

```
$ docker run --privileged \
    --detach \
    --network fn_net \
    --network-alias fn_0 \
    --name fn_0 \
    -e "FN_DB_URL=mysql://func:funcpass@tcp(mysql:3306)/fn_db" \
    fnproject/fnserver
```

Let's start another one, `fn_1`. Basically, this should be done on a separate node (physical or virtual):

```
$ docker run --privileged \
    --detach \
    --network fn_net \
    --network-alias fn_1 \
    --name fn_1 \
    -e "FN_DB_URL=mysql://func:funcpass@tcp(mysql:3306)/fn_db" \
    fnproject/fnserver
```

Well, after setting all Fn Server instances, now it's time to aggregate them. We use Fn LB to act as the load balancer in front of all the Fn Servers. Similar to other containers, we just create and attach it to the `fn_net`. As it is the FaaS gateway, we also expose its port to `8080` (from its internal port `8081`) to make the Fn CLI able to connect to the Fn cluster without any special setting. The network alias is just used when we need other services to connect to this gateway.

Next, send a list of Fn Server nodes as the command line.

Currently, the node list configuration is allowed to pass directly to the container only. Just put them in `<name>:<port>` format, separated by a *comma*:

```
$ docker run --detach \
    --network fn_net \
    --network-alias fnlb \
    --name fnlb \
    -p 8080:8081 \
    fnproject/fnlb:latest --nodes fn_0:8080,fn_1:8080
```

OK, now it's time to verify that everything is up and running. We double-check all containers with the `docker ps` command:

```
$ docker ps --format "table {{.ID}}\t{{.Names}}\t{{.Command}}\t{{.Ports}}"
CONTAINER ID    NAMES      COMMAND                  PORTS
ce4f8e9bc300    fnlb       "./fnlb --nodes fn_0..."   0.0.0.0:8080->8081/tcp
dae4fb892b4d    fn_1       "preentry.sh ./fnser..."   2375/tcp
8aefeb9e19ef    fn_0       "preentry.sh ./fnser..."   2375/tcp
67bd136c331a    mysql      "docker-entrypoint.s..."   3306/tcp
```

In the next two sections, we will cover how to monitor what's happening with Fn UI and how to see and maybe further analyze the logs stored in the database.

Monitoring with Fn UI

Fn UI is the user interface project created for Fn. It provides a simple dashboard with easy-to-use time series graphs to monitor how functions are doing in near real time. To start the Fn UI, we create and attach the container to the `fn_net`, also with the port published to `4000`. The Fn UI requires the URL of an Fn Server. But all of them are behind the Fn LB, so we just set `FN_API_URL` to the Fn LB location.

Please note that they are all connected to each other inside the `fn_net` network, so the URL appears to be `http://fnlb:8081`, using the real name and port of `fnlb` inside the network:

```
$ docker run --detach \
    --network fn_net \
    --network-alias fnui \
    -p 4000:4000 \
    -e "FN_API_URL=http://fnlb:8081" fnproject/ui
```

After setting up the Fn UI instance, browse to `localhost:8080` to open the dashboard. We will see all applications listed there, as shown in the following screenshot. An application could be managed, such as creating or deleting, there too. If you do not want the screen to be always auto refreshing, uncheck **Auto refresh**:

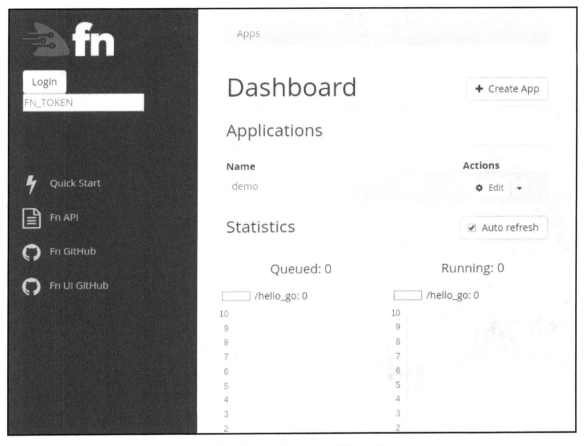

Figure 5.5: An Fn dashboard showing the list of Fn applications

After selecting an application, you can execute a function within the dashboard by clicking the **Run Function** button, as in the following screenshot. If an error occurs when executing the function and it fails, for example, a notification will pop up as in the following example.

To execute the function, put the **Payload** in the form of JSON and press the **Run** button:

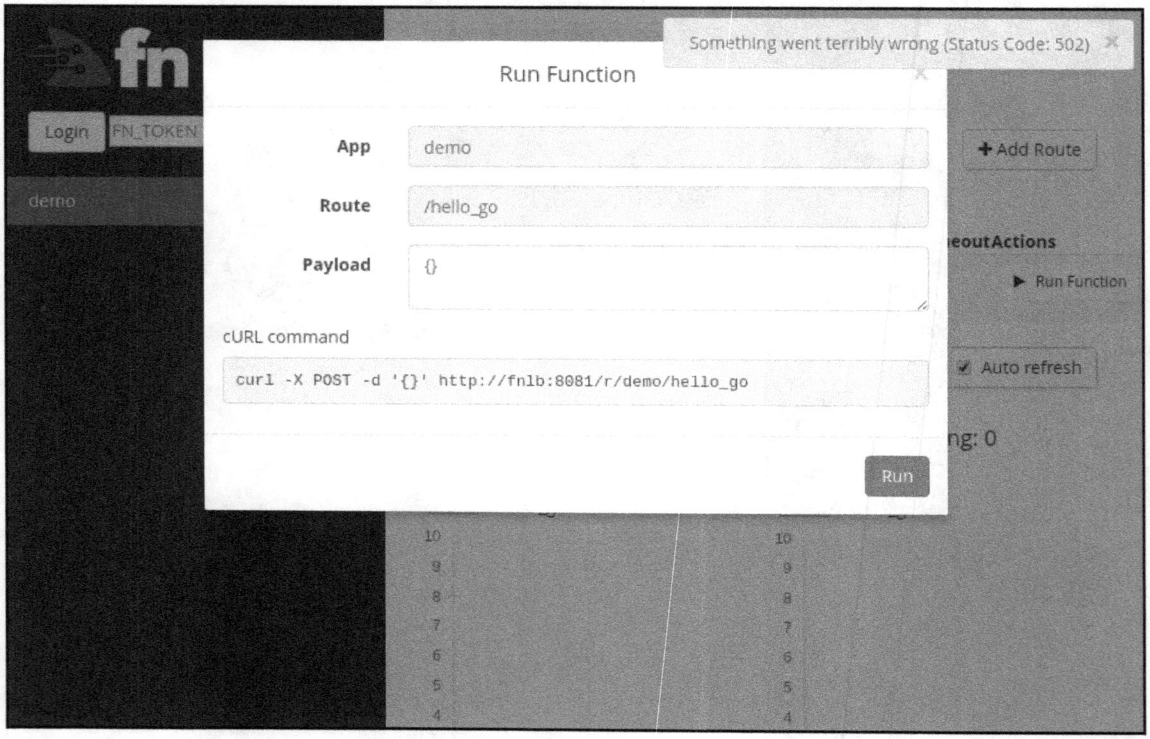

Figure 5.6: A dialog for invoking functions

When a function invocation is completed, its name and count will appear in the **Completed** graph. Here's the `curl` command to invoke the function. Run it multiple times to see the graph change:

```
$ curl -X POST -d '{"Name":"chanwit"}'
http://localhost:8080/r/demo/hello_go
```

There is also the **Running** graph that displays the number of functions still running in parallel. The following screenshot shows these graphs in action:

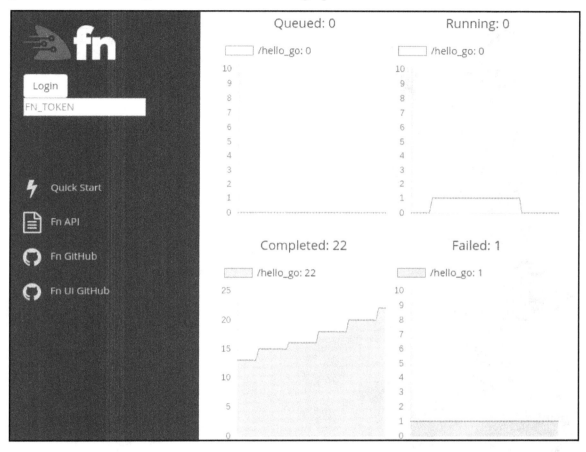

Figure 5.7: Graphs displaying different states of Fn's functions

Let's see what will happen when we run a number of requests with invalid inputs. Here's the command:

```
$ curl -X POST -d '' http://localhost:8080/r/demo/hello_go
```

With this, the `hello_go` function will exit with code `250` and appear in the **Failed** graph. We run it repeatedly to make the number of failure going up, as seen in the following screenshot:

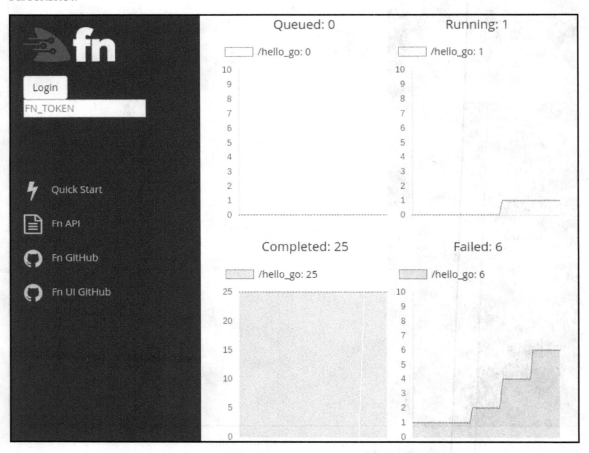

Figure 5.8: The bottom right-hand graph showing the increment numbers of failed functions

We now already know how to use the Fn UI to monitor the function invocation. Next, we will use a simple DBMS UI to help browse the logs collected by Fn Servers.

Viewing call logs with MyAdmin

With MySQL as the central Log Store, we can simply access MySQL with any tool to query or event analyze the logs. In this example, we use a simple MyAdmin UI to connect to the MySQL backend. Here's the `docker run` command to start MyAdmin.

We just simply attach an instance of MyAdmin to the same network and tell MyAdmin to connect to `mysql`, the service name of the backend DB:

```
$ docker run --detach \
    --name myadmin \
    --network fn_net \
    --network-alias myadmin \
    -p 9000:80 \
    -e PMA_HOST=mysql \
    phpmyadmin/phpmyadmin
```

Browse to the exposed port, in this example port number `9000`, and log in using **Username** and **Password**, set during the setup of MySQL (`func`/`funcpass`). The following screenshot shows the login page of **phpMyAdmin**:

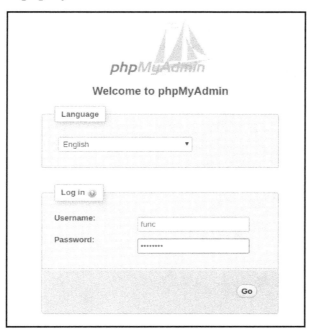

Figure 5.9: The login page of phpMyAdmin that will connect to the Fn's log database

Inside the **phpMyAdmin** panel, take a look at the `fn_db` parameter and we will see all the tables for storing Fn information, as shown in the following screenshot. The data of the table `apps` are created by the command `fn apps create`, for example. What we'd like to see are table `calls` and table `logs`. The content of table `calls` can be retrieved by the `fn calls list`, and the content of table `logs` can also be retrieved in a similar way using `fn logs get`. But when we are able to access the `logs` directly, we can even do some analysis directly with the available data:

Figure 5.10: The list of all Fn's tables in phpMyAdmin

The following screenshot shows the content of table `calls`. There is a **status** column, which allows us to effectively filter to see what the call (**status**) is: **success** or **error**. There is also the stats column, which contains some temporal information to be retrieved and displayed by the Fn UI:

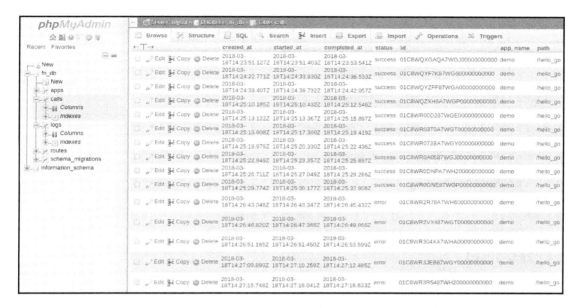

Figure 5.11: Fn calls log data in table calls

The following screenshot shows table `logs`. In the `logs` table, it just stamps each entry with the call ID. The column **log** shows the log message we printed out to the STDERR. We can see that there are different incorrect behaviors just by trying to send some invalid inputs to our `hello_go` function. With this table being so accessible, we can troubleshoot the Fn functions effectively without installing other extra tools:

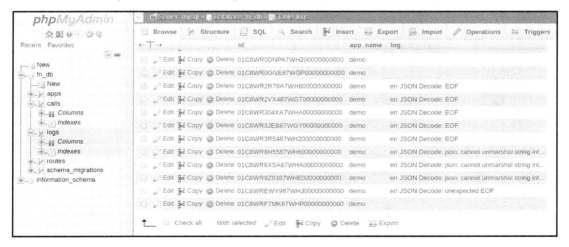

Figure 5.12: Fn logs data captured from a function's STDERR

OK, it seems everything is working correctly if we could get MyAdmin to show the logs data. Finally, to confirm that all containers are running and what they should look like, just use the `docker ps` command again to check all running containers:

```
$ docker ps --format "table {{.ID}}\t{{.Names}}\t{{.Command}}\t{{.Ports}}"
CONTAINER ID      NAMES       COMMAND                  PORTS
70810f341284      fnui        "npm start"              0.0.0.0:4000->4000/tcp
ce4f8e9bc300      fnlb        "./fnlb --nodes fn_0..."  0.0.0.0:8080->8081/tcp
dae4fb892b4d      fn_1        "preentry.sh ./fnser..."  2375/tcp
8aefeb9e19ef      fn_0        "preentry.sh ./fnser..."  2375/tcp
8645116af77d      myadmin     "/run.sh phpmyadmin"     9000/tcp,
0.0.0.0:9000->80/tcp
67bd136c331a      mysql       "docker-entrypoint.s..."  3306/tcp
```

Exercise

Now it's time to review all the things in this chapter:

1. What does the Fn architecture look like?
2. How is the architecture different from other FaaS platforms?
3. What is the role of the Fn Server?
4. How can we configure an Fn Server to use an external data store?
5. What is the difference between the techniques used by the Fn's Java runtime and Go runtime?
6. How are an application and routes organized?
7. What is the role of Fn LB?
8. What is the role of the Fn UI?
9. How can we see the results of previous calls?
10. How can we examine the log messages of a failed invocation?
11. Describe how an Fn function interacts with STDIN, STDOUT, and STDERR?

Summary

This chapter discussed the Fn Project, its components, and architecture. We started using Fn with its command line, the Fn CLI.

We then discussed the structure of an Fn function, such as how it interacts with STDIN, STDOUT, and STDERR. We learned how to build and deploy Fn functions, both with Java and Go runtimes.

Then we formed an Fn cluster on Docker Swarm and linked the Fn Server instances to an external DB store, MySQL. We load balanced the Fn instances using Fn LB, a load balancer specifically implemented by the same team.

With the Fn UI, we learned how to use it to monitor invocations for Fn. With MyAdmin, we used it to browse calls and error logs directly in MySQL. A simple tool like MyAdmin could be used to achieve the same analytical result without preparing a complex toolchain.

The next chapter will introduce OpenWhisk, another serverless stack from the Apache project, and those used by IBM to offer serverless services in their cloud.

6
OpenWhisk on Docker

This chapter will discuss another player in the serverless space, OpenWhisk. The chapter will start with an overview of the OpenWhisk platform, its design rationale, and features. After that, the chapter will go through the steps of deploying a local instance of OpenWhisk for function development, how to use its command-line interface, its components and architecture, and how to prepare functions to deploy on the platform.

What is OpenWhisk?

Donated to the Apache foundation, OpenWhisk is a robust FaaS platform originally developed by IBM and Adobe. Built atop Docker container technologies, OpenWhisk can be deployed in the cloud or on on-premises hardware. It is a platform that frees developers from worrying about managing the life cycle of their code or operations of the container runtimes that execute the code. OpenWhisk is designed to be scalable and to support massive numbers of function invocations. Currently, OpenWhisk is the engine behind IBM Cloud Functions.

The OpenWhisk scaling mechanism is not built on top of Docker Swarm or Kubernetes schedulers. It plugs directly into each Docker instance to start and scale function containers. With this design, OpenWhisk fits better with the plain Docker infrastructure than Kubernetes.

For developers, OpenWhisk provides a number of compelling features via its high-level programming model surrounding functions. Its event triggering mechanism is shown in Figure 6.1:

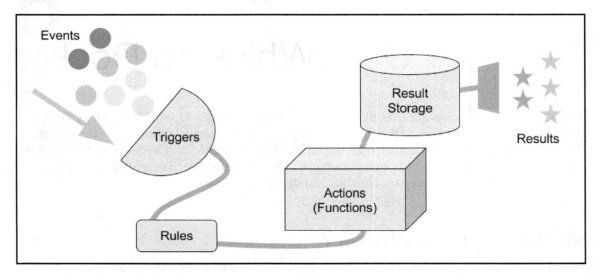

Figure 6.1: OpenWhisk's flow of event triggering

Similar to other platforms, OpenWhisk's smallest deployment unit is a function. In OpenWhisk, a function is referred to as an action. An action can be executed in response to an event. An event, in the form of a trigger, will be processed through a rule, where it selects an appropriate action to execute. After the action is executed, its result will be stored in the result storage before being emitted back to the source of the event.

OpenWhisk natively supports many language runtimes out of the box. However, this chapter focuses only on its Docker runtime, which allows developers to pack any kind of workload into a container and let OpenWhisk do the rest. An action in OpenWhisk can be invoked synchronously, asynchronously, or even on a schedule. Besides an action, OpenWhisk provides a declarative programming construct, such as a sequence to allow multiple actions to be chained and executed as a flow.

Installing OpenWhisk

At the time of writing, the quickest way to install OpenWhisk on a local machine is to use Docker and Docker Compose.

To install Docker Compose, we can follow instructions from `https://github.com/docker/compose/releases`:

```
$ sudo curl -L
https://github.com/docker/compose/releases/download/1.17.1/docker-compose-`
uname -s`-`uname -m` -o /usr/local/bin/docker-compose
$ sudo chmod +x /usr/local/bin/docker-compose
```

To check the version of Docker Compose, use the following command:

```
$ docker-compose --version
docker-compose version 1.17.1, build 6d101fb
```

We use Docker Compose 1.17.1 in this chapter.

Also check if the Git is installed already. If so, now we are ready to install a local OpenWhisk instance.

First, clone the OpenWhisk Dev tools repository from GitHub (`https://github.com/apache/incubator-openwhisk-devtools`) using the following command:

```
$ git clone --depth=1
https://github.com/apache/incubator-openwhisk-devtools
```

The `--depth=1` tells `git` to shallow clone the repository, which means that only the latest revision of the Git history will be there to save time and space.

Next, move into the directory `incubator-openwhisk-devtools/docker-compose`. This directory contains `docker-compose.yml` and the required environment variables to start a single node OpenWhisk instance. Look for a `Makefile` there; it contains the `quick-start` target to provision an instance, set up the initial data, and invoke an example function:

```
$ make quick-start
```

The command will be doing the following.

First, it will download the latest source of OpenWhisk from the `master` branch of its GitHub repository, along with the `wsk` CLI binary. Second, it will start an OpenWhisk local cluster and initialize the data with the Ansible playbooks that came with the OpenWhisk source tree. Then it will register the `hello-world` function and finally invoke it:

```
Response body size is 9 bytes
Response body received:
["guest"]
ok: whisk auth set. Run 'wsk property get --auth' to see the new value.
ok: whisk API host set to 192.168.1.40:443
ok: whisk namespace set to guest
waiting for the Whisk invoker to come up ...
creating the hello.js function ...
invoking the hello-world function ...
adding the function to whisk ...
ok: created action hello
invoking the function ...
invocation result: { "payload": "Hello, World!" }
{ "payload": "Hello, World!" }
deleting the function ...
ok: deleted action hello
To invoke the function again use: make hello-world
To stop openwhisk use: make destroy
```

Sometimes, when the process is up and running, the instance becomes flaky. Simply press *Ctrl + C* and issue the command `make run` instead of `make quick-start` to try to start the instance again. If you'd like to start over, simply run the `make destroy` command to destroy the instance. After destroying it, you can start over with `make quick-start`.

If the output ends like this, OpenWhisk is now ready to serve at `localhost:443`:

```
Response body received:
["guest"]
ok: whisk auth set. Run 'wsk property get --auth' to see the new value.
ok: whisk API host set to localhost:443
ok: whisk namespace set to guest
```

We can then use the `docker ps` command to double check that all OpenWhisk containers are running:

```
$ docker ps --format "table {{.ID}}\t{{.Image}}"
CONTAINER ID    IMAGE
5e44dca4c542    openwhisk/nodejs6action:latest
d784018ef3de    adobeapiplatform/apigateway:1.1.0
74b6b1d71510    openwhisk/controller
0c0cb4779412    openwhisk/invoker
```

```
b0111898e1a8    nginx:latest
874dac58a7c1    landoop/kafka-topics-ui:0.9.3
611e9b97ad74    confluentinc/cp-kafka-rest:3.3.1
4e1a82df737e    wurstmeister/kafka:0.11.0.1
9c490336abff    redis:2.8
abc4c0845fac    couchdb:1.6
451ab4c7bf45    zookeeper:3.4
```

Using the wsk client

The wsk client will have already been installed by the make quick-start command. The wsk binary can be found at openmaster/bin/wsk. We usually copy the wsk CLI to /usr/local/bin and set up bash completion for it:

```
$ sudo cp openwhisk-master/bin/wsk /usr/local/bin

$ wsk sdk install bashauto
The bash auto-completion script (wsk_cli_bash_completion.sh) is installed
in the current directory.
To enable command line completion of wsk commands, source the auto
completion script into your bash environment

$ source wsk_cli_bash_completion.sh
$ wsk
```

```
Usage:
  wsk [command]

...
```

The first sub-command introduced here is `wsk property get`. It is to display OpenWhisk information, including the current namespace, the authentication key, and the build number. For example, we use `-i` or `--insecure` for insecurely connecting to the OpenWhisk instance as the generated certificate is self-signed:

```
$ wsk -i property get
client cert
Client key
whisk auth
23bc46b1-71f6-4ed5-8c54-816aa4f8c502:123zO3xZCLrMN6v2BKK1dXYFpXlPkccOFqm12C
dAsMgRU4VrNZ91yGVCGuMDGIwP
whisk API host          localhost:443
whisk API version       v1
whisk namespace         guest
whisk CLI version       2017-12-05T00:51:32+00:00
whisk API build         "09/01/2016"
whisk API build number  "latest"
```

What does the information tell us? We are currently at the guest `namespace` using API version 1 and the long string, starting with `23bc`, is our API key for authentication. Any OpenWhisk client, including the `wsk` itself, needs this key to connect to the OpenWhisk instance. Our current API gateway is at `localhost:443`, which will forward all requests to the underlying controllers. The overview of each OpenWhisk component and the architecture will be discussed in the next section.

Components and architecture

In this section, we discuss the architecture and components of OpenWhisk. OpenWhisk is designed to be a rock-solid FaaS platform as it is powering IBM Cloud Function, one of the FaaS production systems already launched by IBM. The key of this rock-solid architecture is Kafka. OpenWhisk cleverly uses Kafka as its backbone to guarantee that every single function request accepted by Kafka will be delivered to the invoker layer. Let's start by looking its overall architecture.

Architecture

The following diagram in *Figure 6.2* shows the overall architecture of OpenWhisk:

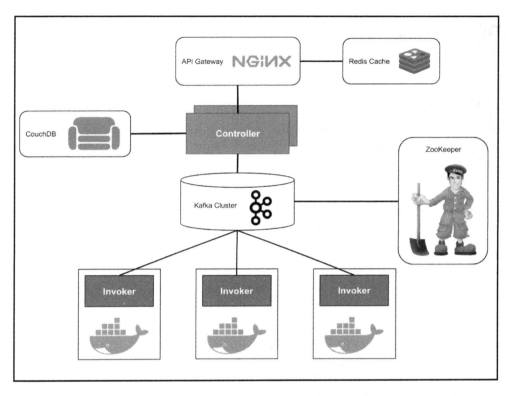

Figure 6.2: The overview architecture of OpenWhisk.

The edge component is the API gateway built on top of NGINX and OpenResty. The API gateway optionally uses Redis for caching. The API gateway sits in front of one or more controllers. The controller stores all configuration in a CouchDB cluster. Behind the controller, there is a Kafka cluster coordinated by a ZooKeeper quorum. The Kafka cluster is very important; every invocation is guaranteed to be executed. Kafka acts as a resilient buffer between controllers and invokers. Each invoker is responsible for invoking real implementations of functions, in this case Docker containers. Therefore, an invoker requires a special privilege to connect to the host's Docker socket. An invoker is optionally able to use `docker-runc` to improve the performance of the invocation process. Every single component of OpenWhisk is able to run inside a container, such as when we deployed it with Docker Compose.

Components

Now we will proceed to the details of each component.

API gateway

The API gateway component of OpenWhisk is built atop NGINX and OpenResty technologies. The main reason NGINX is chosen is because it provides high performance as the edge component of the platform. NGINX sits in front of every other component in the system. The API gateway is capable of caching the request with OpenResty talking to a Redis cluster on its side. However, Redis is an optional component. It can easily be disabled by removing it from the Docker Compose configuration. The API gateway is also responsible for severing the secured HTTPS protocol from users.

The current version of the API gateway is `adobeapiplatform/apigateway:1.1.0`. It is the version of the API gateway under joint development by Adobe and IBM.

Controller

A controller is one of the most important components of OpenWhisk. As the name implies, it mainly controls the invocation process of the cluster. Controllers can work without having the API gateway in front of them. A controller serves the HTTP protocol directly, in an insecure form, as the HTTPS part is the function of the API gateway. Basically, a controller source is a part of the OpenWhisk project. The configuration used in this chapter is the latest Docker image published by OpenWhisk.

Database

The storage component of OpenWhisk is CouchDB. CouchDB is highly available, document-based data storage. The controller talks to CouchDB to store every entity related to the function invocation. The most important entity stored in CouchDB is the activation data. The activation data contains information of each invocation process. The progress of actions and their results are stored in the form of *activation documents*.

The official CouchDB version 1.6, `couchdb:1.6`, is used in the current configuration.

Kafka

Kafka plays a very important role in the system. By nature, Kafka is a message broker that stores every received message and replays them reliably. With Kafka as the backbone, requests for action invocation will be reliably delivered to the invokers.

Kafka is formed as a cluster using the ZooKeeper quorum. Kafka is running on port `9092` within the default network. We use the `wurstmeister/kafka:0.11.0.1` image for the configuration in this chapter.

Invoker

The invoker is the component that is responsible for receiving invocation requests from Kafka topics, message queues that consumers could subscribe to receive messages. After receiving the messages, the invoker executes the functions using a backend runtime. OpenWhisk supports both native and Docker runtimes. The Docker runtime is internally called **blackbox**.

OpenWhisk also has an option to use Docker's `runc` directly to improve the function performance. With this architecture, the invoker requires access to `/var/run/docker.sock` of the local Docker host. This limitation prevents OpenWhisk from scaling efficiently in Swarm mode. We will discuss the new architecture for OpenWhisk over Swarm in a later chapter, when we discuss the deployment of OpenWhisk in a production environment.

Action runtime

There are several kinds of runtime provided by OpenWhisk. Java, Node.js, and Python are native runtimes, for example. As previously mentioned, the Docker runtime is called blackbox.

The runtime takes the Docker image registered by the process of action creation. Then it starts the Docker container to accept the request. The runtime can keep the container running so subsequent calls can be significantly faster.

Function preparation

In this section, we discuss how to prepare a function using the Docker template called **Docker skeleton**, provided by OpenWhisk.

OpenWhisk Docker SDK

To install the Docker skeleton, normally we would do the following:

```
$ wsk -i sdk install docker
```

But if the file does not exist on your local OpenWhisk, you can download it directly from https://github.com/apache/incubator-openwhisk-runtime-docker/releases/download/sdk%400.1.0/blackbox-0.1.0.tar.gz.

The following steps are to download SDK, extract the SDK, change its directory from dockerSkeleton to docker_c, and change into the docker_c directory to check its contents:

```
$ curl -sSL -O
https://github.com/apache/incubator-openwhisk-runtime-docker/releases/downl
oad/sdk%400.1.0/blackbox-0.1.0.tar.gz
$ tar xf blackbox-0.1.0.tar.gz
$ mv dockerSkeleton docker_c
$ cd docker_c
$ ls
buildAndPush.sh Dockerfile example.c README.md
```

The skeleton contains a Dockerfile, a simple C program, a bash script for building and pushing the finished function to Docker's Hub, and a README.md file.

We start with the content of the C program to see what it is for. The C program that came with the Docker skeleton SDK contains only the main function with a couple of printf statements:

```c
#include <stdio.h>

int main(int argc, char *argv[]) {
    printf("This is a log message from an arbitrary C program!\n");
    printf("{ \"msg\": \"Hello from C program!\", \"args\": %s }",
      (argc == 1) ? "undefined" : argv[1]);
}
```

The last printf line tells us the whole story of OpenWhisk's action. This action returns JSON data by printing it out to STDOUT. The action accepts arguments, also in the form of JSON, through the main function's argv. It is the action's responsibility to decode the arguments and encode the output.

Next, we'll take a look at its Dockerfile.

The file starts by declaring `openwhisk/dockerskeleton` as the base image. In the next line, the environment variable `FLASK_PROXY_PORT` is defined as `8080`. You may guess here that the framework used as the wrapper of every Docker function is `Flask`, a Python web framework.

Moving to the next two lines, they add the C program into the building container, install the GCC compiler, and then compile the program. The output binary is named `exec`. It must be placed at `/action/exec`. This is the mandatory location of the executable needed by OpenWhisk's `actionproxy`.

What is `actionproxy`? It is the OpenWhisk version of a function wrapping server. The server accepts a web request through its exposed port, `8080`. As mentioned earlier, it is written in Python with the Flask framework, so every OpenWhisk function requires Python and Flask dependencies in order to start the `actionproxy`. This kind of setup is already there by inheriting from the base image, `openwhisk/dockerskeleton`:

```
# Dockerfile for example whisk docker action
FROM openwhisk/dockerskeleton

ENV FLASK_PROXY_PORT 8080

### Add source file(s)
ADD example.c /action/example.c

RUN apk add --no-cache --virtual .build-deps \
        bzip2-dev \
        gcc \
        libc-dev \
### Compile source file(s)
 && cd /action; gcc -o exec example.c \
 && apk del .build-deps

CMD ["/bin/bash", "-c", "cd actionProxy && python -u actionproxy.py"]
```

Instead of using the provided script, we will build it ourselves using the `docker build` command. Please recall that you need to use your own `<DOCKER ID>` as the repository name to allow you to push the built image onto Docker Hub:

```
$ docker build -t chanwit/whisk_c .

Sending build context to Docker daemon 6.656kB
Step 1/5 : FROM openwhisk/dockerskeleton
latest: Pulling from openwhisk/dockerskeleton
...
 ---> 25d1878c2f31
```

```
Step 2/5 : ENV FLASK_PROXY_PORT 8080
 ---> Running in 932e3e3d6c0b
 ---> 647789067bf0
Removing intermediate container 932e3e3d6c0b
Step 3/5 : ADD example.c /action/example.c
 ---> 91eb99956da2
Step 4/5 : RUN apk add --no-cache --virtual .build-deps bzip2-dev gcc
       libc-dev && cd /action; gcc -o exec example.c && apk del .build-deps
 ---> Running in 943930981ac6
fetch http://dl-cdn.alpinelinux.org/alpine/v3.4/main/x86_64/APKINDEX.tar.gz
fetch
http://dl-cdn.alpinelinux.org/alpine/v3.4/community/x86_64/APKINDEX.tar.gz
(1/19) Upgrading musl (1.1.14-r15 -> 1.1.14-r16)
...
(17/17) Purging libgcc (5.3.0-r0)
Executing busybox-1.24.2-r13.trigger
OK: 32 MiB in 35 packages
 ---> d1cc0ed0f307
Removing intermediate container 943930981ac6
Step 5/5 : CMD /bin/bash -c cd actionProxy && python -u actionproxy.py
 ---> Running in fc68fc0ba06f
 ---> 924277b2a3a0
Removing intermediate container fc68fc0ba06f
Successfully built 924277b2a3a0
Successfully tagged chanwit/whisk_c:latest
```

If everything was done correctly, don't forget to use the `docker push` command to store this image on the Hub.

Preparing a Go function

Next, we will write a function using the Go programming language to show you how to decode JSON parameters using the Go built-in library. Of course, we will modify OpenWhisk's Docker skeleton by adding Go compilers and use a multi-stage build to optimize the build process.

Let's start over.

We'll untar the Docker skeleton again, and this time we rename the `dockerSkeleton` directory `docker_go`:

```
$ tar xf blackbox-0.1.0.tar.gz
$ mv dockerSkeleton docker_go
$ cd docker_go
```

Inside the `docker_go` directory, we will write a Go program to decode the JSON `params` of the action, rearrange them, encode them back to JSON, and write them to the caller:

```go
package main

import (
  "encoding/json"
  "fmt"
  "os"
)

func main() {
  rawParams := []byte(os.Args[1])
  params := map[string]string{}

  // decode JSON to a Go map
  err := json.Unmarshal(rawParams, &params)
  if err != nil {
    fmt.Printf(`{"error":%q}`, err.Error())
    os.Exit(0)
  }

  // re-arrange
  keys := []string{}
  values := []string{}
  for k, v := range params {
    keys = append(keys, k)
    values = append(values, v)
  }

  result := map[string]interface{}{
    "message": "Hello from Go",
    "keys": keys,
    "values": values,
  }

  // encode
  rawResult, err := json.Marshal(result)
  if err != nil {
    fmt.Printf(`{"error":%q}`, err.Error())
    os.Exit(0)
  }

  // write JSON back to the caller
  fmt.Print(string(rawResult))
}
```

We save this program as `main.go` before continuing to the next step, writing our Dockerfile for multi-stage builds to compile the Go program, and pack it as an OpenWhisk action. Here's the new version of `Dockerfile`. Its first build stage is to compile the Go program using Go 1.9.2. Please note that we compile it into a statically linked binary so that it can run independently inside the OpenWhisk base image. In the second build stage, we copy the binary `/go/src/app/main` from the first stage as `/action/exec`, the binary location required for OpenWhisk `actionproxy` to execute:

```
# Compile the Go program
FROM golang:1.9.2-alpine3.6

WORKDIR /go/src/app
COPY main.go .

RUN CGO_ENABLED=0 go build -a -ldflags '-extldflags "-static"' main.go

# Build using the base image for whisk docker action
FROM openwhisk/dockerskeleton

ENV FLASK_PROXY_PORT 8080

COPY --from=0 /go/src/app/main /action/exec

CMD ["/bin/bash", "-c", "cd actionProxy && python -u actionproxy.py"]
```

Now the `Dockerfile` is ready. Let's build it using the `docker build` command:

```
$ docker build -t chanwit/whisk_go .
Sending build context to Docker daemon 2.242MB
Step 1/8 : FROM golang:1.9.2-alpine3.6
 ---> bbab7aea1231
Step 2/8 : WORKDIR /go/src/app
 ---> a219190c401f
Removing intermediate container 2a665bded884
Step 3/8 : COPY main.go .
 ---> f0df3a87489d
Step 4/8 : RUN CGO_ENABLED=0 go build -a -ldflags '-extldflags "-static"'
main.go
 ---> Running in ec72e6f59a57
 ---> e0f943bac9a5
Removing intermediate container ec72e6f59a57
Step 5/8 : FROM openwhisk/dockerskeleton
 ---> 25d1878c2f31
Step 6/8 : ENV FLASK_PROXY_PORT 8080
 ---> Running in 846db07a0f5b
 ---> 543e673a9c79
```

```
Removing intermediate container 846db07a0f5b
Step 7/8 : COPY --from=0 /go/src/app/main /action/exec
 ---> 8ec5987098d8
Step 8/8 : CMD /bin/bash -c cd actionProxy && python -u actionproxy.py
 ---> Running in ea25c9a65bcc
 ---> a4193ccd5f48
Removing intermediate container ea25c9a65bcc
Successfully built a4193ccd5f48
Successfully tagged chanwit/whisk_go:latest
```

The action image is now ready as `chanwit/whisk_go`. Again, please use your Docker Hub's ID, not mine, as the image repository and don't forget to push it to the Hub.

Invoking functions

This section describes the internal flow of how OpenWhisk invokes its actions. We will learn how to create (or register) a Docker container as an OpenWhisk action and how to invoke it.

Invocation flows

As OpenWhisk is an event-driven platform, any kind of event fired to it could be intercepted and interpreted. However, in this example, we will show you only the event triggered by sending a direct request to the gateway.

The invocation flow starts with an invocation request in the form of an HTTP-based request and is sent to the API gateway. For example, we can use the wsk CLI to initiate this kind of request. After the API gateway receives the request, it will forward that call to a controller behind it.

One of the most important components of OpenWhisk is the controller. The controller is a component written in Scala using the infamous framework Akka and Spray to implement a set of REST APIs. The controller accepts all kinds of requests; if it accepts a POST request, it will interpret it as an invocation of an OpenWhisk action.

The controller then starts to authenticate and authorize the access of the requested action.

The controller will look up the credential information and verify it against the data stored in an instance of CouchDB.

If the action is not found, the controller simply returns 404 back to the caller, for example. Also, if access is denied after verification of the credentials, the controller will send a chunk of JSON back to the caller saying that they are not allowed to access the action.

If everything is granted, the controller goes to the next step.

The controller then again looks up the information about the action: what it is, what kind it is, and how to invoke it.

In our case, we use Docker as an action primitive. So, the controller will find that our action is a blackbox. Now it's ready to invoke the action.

The controller will not make a request to an invoker directly; instead, it will make a request to a Kafka cluster, the backbone of the messaging system. As previously mentioned, using Kafka could prevent the loss of the invocation, as well as make the system robust by queuing the invocation when the system is busy under heavy load.

So the controller publishes a message to Kafka. The request message contains all information needed to invoke an action. This message is also persisted by Kafka so that it can be replayed when the system crashes.

Once Kafka gets the message, the controller is responded to with an activation ID to later obtain the result of invocation.

On the other side of Kafka, a set of invokers subscribe to the requested messages. Once a message is available in the queue, an invoker will be notified. Then the invoker will do the real job, invoking the real Docker container. After it gets the results, the invoker stores them in the instance of CouchDB under the same activation ID.

Action invoke

OK, now we are ready to try out both newly created C and Go functions built in the previous sections. First, we will create an action using the `wsk action create` command starting with the C program:

```
$ wsk -i action create --docker chanwit/whisk_c whisk_c
ok: created action whisk_c
```

If things go correctly, `wsk` will tell us `ok: created action`. Next, we will invoke the action using the `wsk action invoke` command. The `invoke` command accepts one or more `--param` to pass parameters to the action. We can also pass `--result` to obtain the result synchronously. The result is, of course returned as JSON:

```
$ wsk -i action invoke --param key value --result whisk_c
{
    "args": {
        "key": "value"
    },
    "msg": "Hello from C program!"
}
```

We will try once more, this time with the Go program. First, create the action:

```
$ wsk -i action create --docker chanwit/whisk_go whisk_go
ok: created action whisk_go
```

Then, invoke the action using `wsk action invoke`:

```
$ wsk -i action invoke --param hello world --result whisk_go
{
    "keys": [
        "hello"
    ],
    "message": "Hello from Go",
    "values": [
        "world"
    ]
}
```

As we have seen, we pack actions with Docker and it basically simplifies the whole process, starting with action preparation, creation, and invocation.

Obtaining activation results

Each time an action is invoked, OpenWhisk creates an activation record for it. To see the activation record, we may invoke an action without the `--result` parameter, for example:

```
$ wsk -i action invoke --param hello world whisk_go
ok: invoked /guest/whisk_go with id 6ba2c0fd6f4348b8a2c0fd6f4388b864
```

The ID `6ba2c0fd6f4348b8a2c0fd6f4388b864` is called an activation ID. We can now obtain the activation record using the `wsk activation get` command. Putting a field name after the activation ID will filter it to display only that field. The following example shows only the field `response` of the activation record `6ba2c0`:

```
$ wsk -i activation get 6ba2c0fd6f4348b8a2c0fd6f4388b864 response
ok: got activation 6ba2c0fd6f4348b8a2c0fd6f4388b864, displaying field
response
{
    "status": "success",
    "statusCode": 0,
    "success": true,
    "result": {
        "keys": [
            "hello"
        ],
        "message": "Hello from Go",
        "values": [
            "world"
        ]
    }
}
```

In the activation record, the JSON result is placed under the `result` key. You may observe that all the data is correctly serialized to JSON and recorded there.

User interface

There is no open source portal for OpenWhisk at the time of writing. To make it easier for developers to use OpenWhisk, I'm developing a UI portal for it. SuraWhisk is an open source project hosted on GitHub. Its source can be found at `https://github.com/surawhisk/ui`. If you do not want to look at the source code, you can just start the UI from a ready-to-use Docker image.

First, create a volume to store the settings data. Endpoints and their API keys for authentication will be stored there in the volume:

```
$ docker volume create surawhisk_vol
```

Then the UI can be run using the following command:

```
$ docker run -d -p 8080:8080 -v surawhisk_vol:/root/data surawhisk/ui
```

After SuraWhisk UI starts, point the browser to `http://localhost:8080`. The UI's navigation bar on the left-hand side currently contains three basic items: settings, actions, and namespaces.

The **Settings** page, as shown in *Figure 6.3*, is for setting up an OpenWhisk endpoint and its API key. The SuraWhisk container is running on a bridge network; therefore, it can access the OpenWhisk's API gateway via the Docker's gateway bridge IP, `172.17.0.1`. That is, the endpoint to our local OpenWhisk's instance will be `https://172.17.0.1/api/v1`. The API key for the current guest namespace can be obtained by running the `wsk` CLI with the following command. If the bridge IP is not working, you may try the local IP of the local machine, as the OpenWhisk's API gateway is exposed over the machine's IP as well:

```
$ wsk property get --auth
whisk auth
23bc46b1-71f6-4ed5-8c54-816aa4f8c502:123zO3xZCLrMN6v2BKK1dXYFpXlPkccOFqm12C
dAsMgRU4VrNZ9lyGVCGuMDGIwP
```

The result of the command provides a long string saying that it is a `whisk auth`. Copy and paste the whole string, `23b...IwP`, into the **API Key** textbox of the **Settings** page, and click the **Save** button:

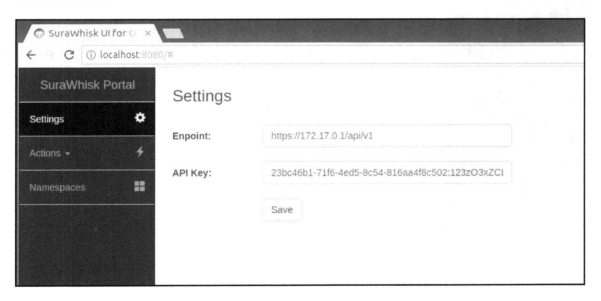

Figure 6.3: The Settings screen of SuraWhisk for specifying the Endpoint and API Key

Now the **SuraWhisk Portal** will be able to communicate with the OpenWhisk instance. We will proceed to the step of defining a new function.

A function, an action in OpenWhisk, can be defined on the **Actions/Create** page, as in *Figure 6.4*. The Docker image built earlier in this chapter will be used here. In the following example, we create a function named `hello` as a Docker container, whose image is `chanwit/whisk_c`:

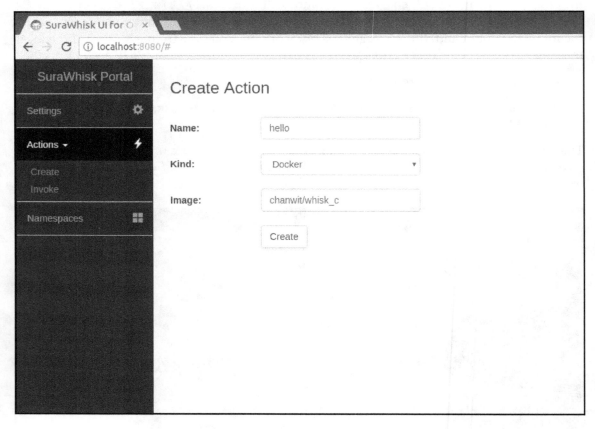

Figure 6.4: The Action Creation screen which allows us to define a new action in OpenWhisk

When everything is ready, click the **Create** button. The portal will connect to the OpenWhisk instance and request creation of a new action. The Docker image is not pulled during this stage, so the step will be finished quickly. If the `hello` action is created successfully, dialog will pop up, as in Figure 6.5.

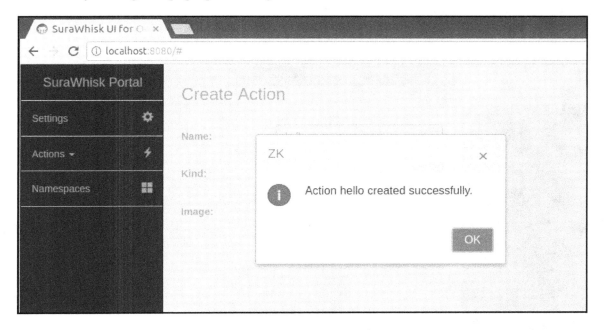

Figure 6.5: Dialog showing that an action was successfully created

To invoke the action, go to the menu **Actions/Invoke** on the left-hand side navigation bar, as in *Figure 6.6*. All actions in the current namespace will be listed in the **Action** combo box. Each invocation accepts key/value pairs as the action's parameters. They can be added by clicking the **Add** button. In the following example, the `book` parameter is set to contain the value `serverless`. A parameter can be removed at any time by clicking the **Remove** button of each pair. These parameters will be encoded into JSON before being passed to the action:

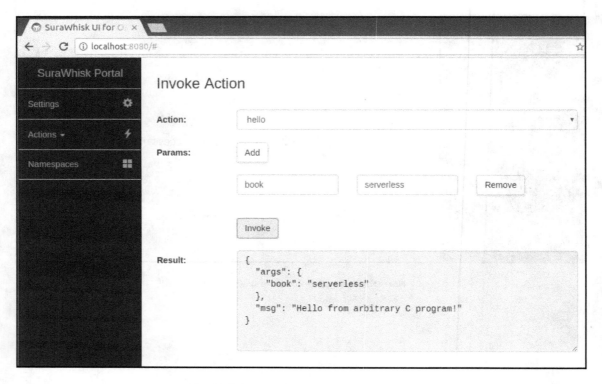

Figure 6.6: The Invoke Action screen in SuraWhisk showing the result

After selecting the action to be invoked, clicking the invoke button will start the invocation process. In the previous example, the `hello` action is in the form of a Docker container.

Exercises

Here are more questions to help you review the contents of this chapter:

1. What are the strengths of OpenWhisk?
2. Please describe OpenWhisk's architecture.
3. What is the role of the OpenWhisk controller?
4. What is the role of Kafka? Why is it important for OpenWhisk?
5. What is an invoker?
6. Is there any reason why the controller and invoker are not connected directly?
7. How could we define and invoke an action on the OpenWhisk platform?
8. How could we improve the performance of the invoker?

Summary

This chapter introduced OpenWhisk, especially when we utilized Docker as parts of its ecosystem. OpenWhisk is a fully featured, fault-tolerant, and polyglot serverless platform that allows you to virtually run functions written in any language.

This chapter walked through its components and architecture, and discussed how to use the `wsk` CLI to prepare, create, and invoke OpenWhisk functions. This chapter also introduced SuraWhisk, a web UI for OpenWhisk to help us manage and invoke OpenWhisk's actions more easily.

We have learned all about three major FaaS platforms. In the next chapter, we will discuss how to prepare and operate a Docker cluster to provision and administrate FaaS platforms on it.

Operating FaaS Clusters

7

One of the hardest things about having a system up and running is administering and maintaining our own clusters. Although serverless is a paradigm aimed at solving this problem entirely, in reality, there are some situations where we still need to provision and take care of servers by ourselves.

The idea behind serverless and Docker is to have a balance between reducing cluster maintenance and administration, and having full control of the cluster. Using Docker is a great way to help balance this.

Along with this balance, the most attractive driving factor for serverless is the *price model*. However, we have found that using Docker on EC2 Spot instances, given the competitive price, is sometimes even cheaper than AWS Lambda or other cloud functions. So with Spot instances, we will get the cheaper price, while our functions will not hit any limitation found in AWS Lambda or others.

Operating Docker-based FaaS clusters uses the same techniques as operating Docker clusters. We need to mix the techniques of running standalone Docker together with the techniques to utilize the Docker Swarm mode. This chapter focuses on *configuration stabilization*, how to prepare the new ingress layer, how to use a network plugin, how to set up the logging system, and how to operate the cluster using Golang scripting.

Stabilizing the configuration

Let's start by carefully stabilizing the cluster configuration. At the time of writing, a Docker cluster works best with the following configuration. *Figure: 7.1* illustrated in this section depicts it well:

- **Ubuntu Server 16.04.3 LTS**: Although Red Hat Linux or CentOS may work best for you, Ubuntu Server is easy to handle. We are constantly informed that Docker has been really well tested with Ubuntu Server. If you choose to use Red Hat or CentOS, please go with version 7.4.
- **Linux Kernel 4.4 LTS**: The 4.4 kernel is an LTS and it's great for Docker. You can also use kernel 4.9 but the kernel, like 4.13, is still too new for Docker.
- **Overlay2 as the Docker storage driver**: Although the **advanced multi-layered unification filesystem (AUFS)** has worked well for Docker for quite a long time, overlay2 should be the new default storage driver for Docker running on the 4.4+ kernel. If you get a chance to run a production cluster on CentOS or RHEL 7.4, overlay2 is also a good option on these distributions.
- **Docker CE 17.06.2 or 17.09.1**: Docker EE 17.06 is also a great option, if you can afford the enterprise edition:

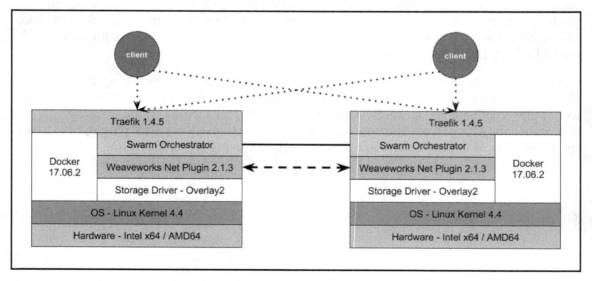

Figure 7.1: A stabilized Docker Swarm stack with Træfik and WeaveWorks network plugin

Choosing the right network plugin

For a long time, people have said that the default Docker overlay network is not great for production. Although the quality of the overlay network driver is getting better and better, we may look at some other network plugins for optimum results. We can replace the default overlay driver with other plugins, for example, WeaveWorks or Contiv. We use WeaveWorks network plugin version 2 in this chapter.

Why WeaveWorks?

The WeaveWorks network plugin for Docker uses the same underlying network implementation as those of Kubernetes CNI. It has also been battle tested by its development team, WeaveWorks Inc. Additionally, it has been working really great so far, on my production clusters.

WeaveWorks network plugin version 2.1.3, in order to avoid disconnection bugs found in the current version of the overlay network driver, it is recommended entirely removing the default ingress network, which is based on the default overlay network driver, in production. A question may be raised here. If the ingress network is removed, we will lose the whole routing mesh, so then how can we route traffic into the cluster? The answer is in the next section.

New ingress and routing

As previously mentioned, we will not use the default Docker *ingress network* for *routing requests* to the running container:

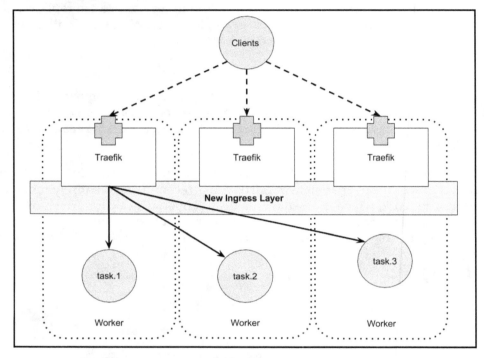

Figure 7.2: The new ingress layer built on top of Træfik, connected to underlying Swarm tasks to form a routing mesh

Yes, we will lose the routing mesh, but we will build our own instead. As shown in the previous figure, we will replace the default routing mesh with a new ingress layer built on top of an L7 load balancer, **Træfik**. You can choose one from the following list of stable versions:

- Træfik v1.4.5 (`traefik@sha256:9c299d9613`)
- Træfik v1.4.6 (`traefik@sha256:89cb51b507`)

The advantage of using Træfik is that the newly built ingress layer is better stabilized. Each service is automatically resolved to be a list of IP addresses by Træfik. So you can choose to use either an IPVS-based load balancer offered by Docker Swarm, or the built-in mechanism offered by Træfik itself.

As Træfik works with the L7 layer, we are additionally allowed to match services with the hostname, and forward the request to a certain task of the matched service. Also, with this new implementation, we could flexibly restart or re-configure the ingress layer on-the-fly without touching the running services. This has been a weak point of the Docker's ingress layer for a very long time.

Tracing component

In the architecture proposed in this book, we use Envoy as a sidecar proxy for every deployed function. With Envoy, it allows distributed trace calling between functions, as in illustrated in the following figure, even if they are prepared by or deployed to different FaaS platforms. This is really an important step for avoiding vendor lock-in. Envoy is compiled and pushed to Docker hub incrementally. We have picked a certain version of Envoy for this book: **EnvoyProxy,**
`envoyproxy/envoy:29989a38c017d3be5aa3c735a797fcf58b754fe5:`

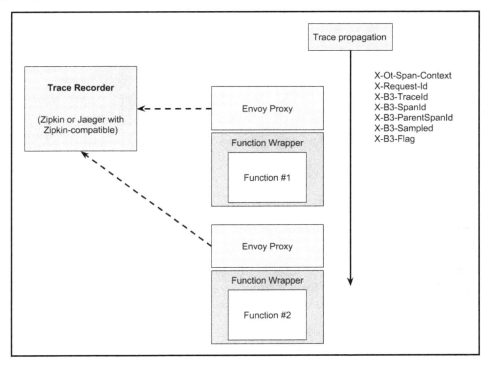

Figure 7.3: A block diagram showing the distributed tracing mechanism with Envoy

The following figure shows two levels of implementation for the sidecar proxy pattern. First, we directly tweak the `Dockerfile` of a function or a service by embedding the **EnvoyProxy** binary into the Docker image. This technique yields the best performance because **EnvoyProxy** talks to the function program through the **loopback** interface inside the container. But when we need to change the configuration of Envoy, such as *retry* or *circuit breaker*, we need to restart the **EnvoyProxy** together with the function instance, shown as the first (**1**) configuration in the following figure:

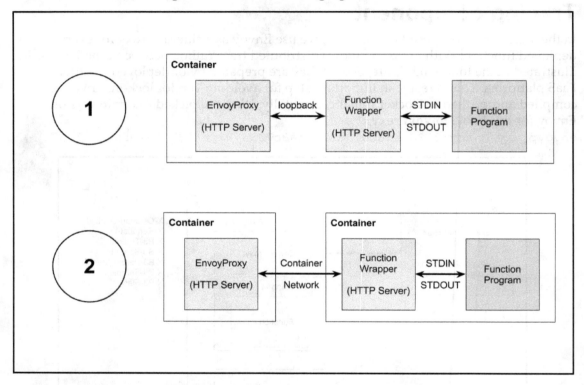

Figure 7.4: Two configurations to implement Envoy as (1) sidecar proxy and (2) edge proxy

So the better configuration when it comes to flexibility and management is the second (**2**) configuration, where we separate **EnvoyProxy**, as an edge proxy, out of the function container. The trade-off here is the network overheads between them.

Retry and circuit breaker

In this section, we discuss one of the most interesting topics to date: the retry and circuit breaker pattern. It would be great to get familiar with this concept before proceeding to implementing a production cluster.

Retry

The problem solved by retry and circuit breaker stems from cascade failures caused by a service or a function inside a chain of calling becoming unavailable. In the following figure, we assume that five different functions or services have 99% availability, so they will fail once every 100 calls. The client observing this service's chain will experience the availability of **A** at only **95.09%**:

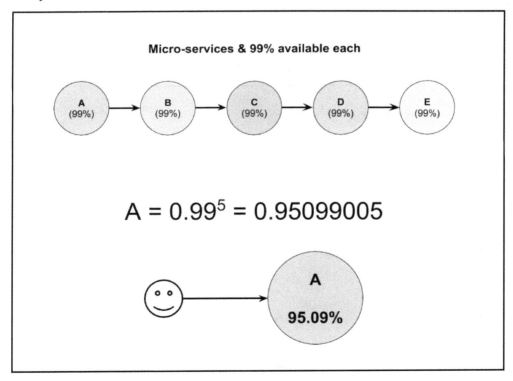

Figure 7.5: A chain of functions or microservices would make their overall availability lower

What does this imply? It means that when this chain becomes eight functions long, the availability will become 92.27%, and if it's 20 functions long, this figure will decrease to 81.79%. To reduce the failure rate, we should retry calling to another instance of function or service when an error, such as HTTP 500, occurs.

But a simple or constant-rate retry is not enough. If we use a simple strategy, our retry calls would increase unnecessary loads to the already broken service. This would cause more problems than it would solve.

Circuit breaker

To resolve this problem, many retry pattern implementations usually come with **Exponential Back-off Retry**. With the exponential back-off strategy, we gradually increase the delay between each retry. For example, we may retry the second call to the service 3 seconds after the fault occurs. If the service still returns an error, we increase the delay to 9 seconds and 27 seconds, for the third and fourth calls respectively. This strategy leaves some room for the service to recover from transient faults. The difference between two kinds of retry strategies is shown in the following figure:

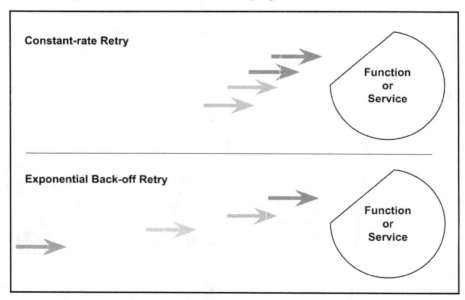

Figure 7.6: The difference between the constant-rate retry and exponential back-off retry strategies

Preparing a production cluster

In this section, we will discuss how to prepare a production Docker Swarm cluster to run FaaS platforms at the cheapest rate possible on AWS Spot instances. The cost of deploying a Docker cluster would be as cheap as running codes on AWS Lambda, but it allows us to control almost everything in our cluster. If the deployment policy is cost-driven, this is the best way to go.

Cost savings with Spot instances

When we are talking about the cloud, its on-demand instances are actually cheap already. However, in the long run, the price of using cloud instances will be similar to buying real machines. To solve this pricing problem, major cloud providers, such as Amazon EC2, and Google Cloud Platform, provide a new instance type, collectively called a **Spot instance** in this book:

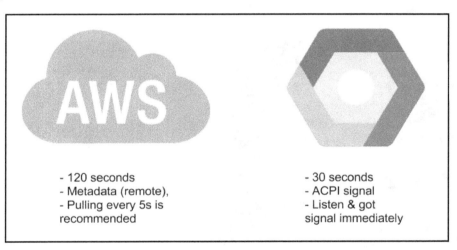

- 120 seconds
- Metadata (remote),
- Pulling every 5s is recommended

- 30 seconds
- ACPI signal
- Listen & got signal immediately

Figure 7.7: Comparison of shutdown signals of a Spot instance on AWS versus Google Cloud

Spot instances are far cheaper than on-demand instances. However, their weak point is the short life cycle and unexpected termination. That is, a Spot instance could be terminated at any time. When it is gone, you have a choice as to whether to preserve or completely discard the volumes. On AWS, the instance will get the notification around 120 seconds before termination via remote metadata, while on Google Cloud, the notification will be sent via an ACPI signal 30 seconds before the machine stops. The rough comparison is shown in the previous figure.

We could put stateless computing to run on these kinds of instances. Both microservices and functions are naturally stateless, so Spot instances fit with the deployment of microservices and functions nicely.

With this kind of infrastructure on cheap instances, its cost will be comparable to AWS Lambda or Google Cloud Functions, but we are more in control of the overall system, meaning no invocation timeout for functions on this kind of infrastructure.

Using EC2 Spot instances

On Amazon EC2, go to `https://aws.amazon.com/ec2/spot/` and we will find the page as shown in the following screenshot. Log onto the AWS Console for Spot instances to set up some of them:

Figure 7.8: The landing page of AWS Spot instances

On the navigation bar, we see **Spot Requests**. Click it to go to the **Spot Requests** screen as shown in the following screenshot. On this screen, clicking **Request Spot Instances** starts the request process:

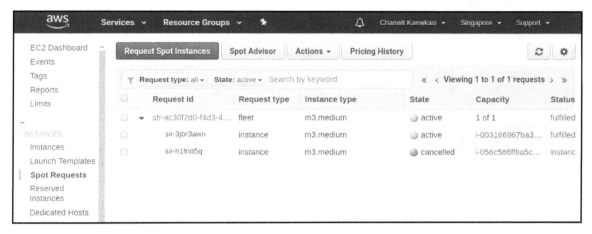

Figure 7.9: The Spot Requests screen on AWS displaying a request with its associated instances

There are three models for requesting Spot instances:

- One-time request. This is one time only, so when the instance is gone, we need to do another request.
- Request a fleet of instances and let AWS maintain the number of target instances. When some instances are terminated, AWS will try its best, depending on our maximum bidding price, to allocate instances to meet the target numbers of each fleet. We have opted for this request model in this chapter.
- Request instances for a fixed period of time. A fixed period is called a **Spot block**, which is between 1 and 6 hours. We will pay more if we set the longer period.

The following diagram shows what the cluster in preparation will look like:

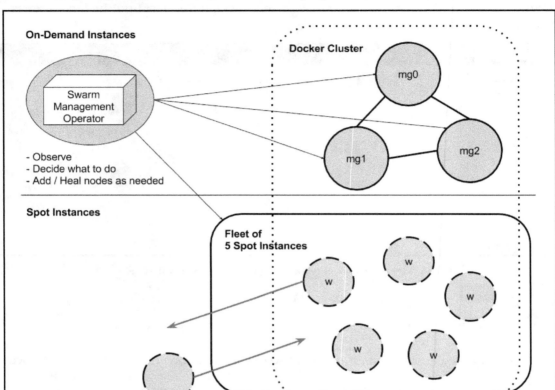

Figure 7.10: A Docker cluster forming on Spot instances using an automatic operator to take care of it

Assume that we already have three boxes provisioned to be managers. To get the cheapest rate possible, it is recommended using three on-demand EC2 nodes as Docker managers, and N-3 Spot instances as Docker workers. We start small with three Spot workers.

 If possible, choose a cloud provider that allows you to create a private network and floating IPs. We will form a Docker cluster on the private network. Most cloud providers allow this, so do not worry.

Let's start

First, SSH into a node we would like to be the first manager, install Docker, and run the `docker swarm init` command on it. The `eth0` is the private network interface provided by the cloud provider. Check yours using the `ip addr` command before proceeding. If you know which interface is the private one, initialize the cluster using the following command:

```
$ docker swarm init --advertise-addr=eth0
```

Next, SSH into the other two nodes. Install Docker and join the cluster using the `docker swarm join` command. Do not forget that we need to use the join token for the *manager*, not for the worker. The token in the following example is the manager token. Please note that my first manager's IP is `172.31.4.52` during this setup. Replace it with your IP address:

```
$ docker swarm join --token
SWMTKN-1-5rvucdwofoam27qownciovd0sngpm31825r2wbdz1jdneiyfyt-
b5bdh4i2jzev4aq4oid1pubi6 172.31.4.52:2377
```

For these first three nodes, do not forget to label them as managers to help you remember.

Here, please make sure that `docker info` shows the list of managers, containing all their private IP addresses. We use `grep -A3` to see the next three lines after the target:

```
$ docker info | grep -A3 "Manager Addresses:"
Manager Addresses:
 172.31.0.153:2377
 172.31.1.223:2377
 172.31.4.52:2377
```

Or, if you are familiar with the `jq` command, try the following:

```
$ docker info --format="{{json .Swarm.RemoteManagers}}" | jq -r .[].Addr
172.31.4.52:2377
172.31.1.223:2377
172.31.0.153:2377
```

The `docker info` command also accepts `--format` to let us customize the output. In the previous example, we used the JSON method provided by the template to generate JSON output. Then we used `jq` to query the IP addresses of all the Swarm managers. The combination of JSON templating and `jq` will be a great tool to build our own set of Docker-based scripts for operating clusters in the long term.

Workers on Spot instances

Then, we will provision another three nodes as a fleet of Spot instances. Here, in the following screenshot, it shows the setup to request a fleet of three Spot instances. Choose the **Request and Maintain** option, then set the **Target capacity** to 3 **instances**:

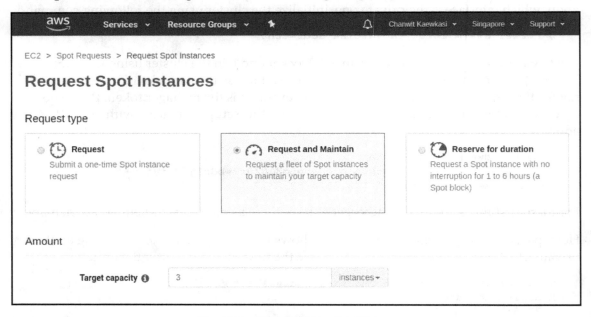

Figure 7.11: Requesting and maintaining a fleet of 3 instances

We configure the setup script to install Docker, join the node to the cluster, and set up the network driver upon the instance creation. The setup must be put into the **User data** section of the fleet setup, as shown in the following screenshot:

Figure 7.12: Putting join instructions into the request's user data

Here's the script used in the **User data** section. Please replace $TOKEN with your worker's token, and $MANAGER_IP with one of your manager's private IP addresses:

```
#!/bin/bash
curl -sSL https://get.docker.com | sh
service docker start
usermod -aG docker ubuntu
docker swarm join --token $TOKEN $MANAGER_IP:2377
docker plugin install --grant-all-permissions weaveworks/net-plugin:2.1.3
```

Now, we wait until the fleet request is fulfilled.

If we get into the first manager, we could check the current nodes in the cluster with the docker node ls command. If everything is OK, we should have six nodes in the cluster:

```
$ docker node ls
ID              HOSTNAME            STATUS   AVAILABILITY   MANAGER STATUS
btul0hbd        ip-172-31-11-209    Ready    Active
etm8veip        ip-172-31-8-157     Ready    Active
iwl4pxnf *      ip-172-31-4-52      Ready    Active         Leader
rsqsflmv        ip-172-31-1-223     Ready    Active         Reachable
uxd36bok        ip-172-31-15-229    Ready    Active
xn7fz2q1        ip-172-31-0-153     Ready    Active         Reachable
```

With this technique, we can easily scale the cluster by simply adjusting the number of Spot instances.

Working with the network plugin

As we can see in the **User data** section in the fleet setup, there will be a line of the script that installs the network plugin for us. It is the WeaveWorks network plugin. The WeaveWorks network plugin uses the information from the `docker info` command to list the IP addresses of all the Swarm managers. The plugin then uses these IP addresses to bootstrap the network mesh.

 The WeaveWorks network plugin must be installed only after you successfully form the set of managers in the cluster.

We use WeaveWorks network plugin 2.1.3. This is the most stable version of it at the time of writing. It is also recommended upgrading to the next minor versions of this plugin, if available.

To install the network plugin, we use the `docker plugin install` command:

```
$ docker plugin install --grant-all-permissions weaveworks/net-plugin:2.1.3
2.1.3: Pulling from weaveworks/net-plugin
82e7025f1f50: Download complete
Digest:
sha256:84e5ff14b54bfb9798a995ddd38956d5c34ddaa4e48f6c0089f6c0e86f1ecfea
Status: Downloaded newer image for weaveworks/net-plugin:2.1.3
Installed plugin weaveworks/net-plugin:2.1.3
```

We use `--grant-all-permissions` just to automate the installation step. Without this parameter, we must manually grant the permissions required by each plugin.

 We need to install a plugin for every single node in the cluster, which means we need to do this six times for our six boxes.

We could check to see whether the network plugin is installed correctly using the following command:

```
$ docker plugin ls
ID                NAME                        DESCRIPTION
ENABLED
f85f0fca2af9  weaveworks/net-plugin:2.1.3  Weave Net plugin for Docker
true
```

The ENABLED status of the plugin will be true, meaning that it is currently active. To check the status of the WeaveWork plugin and its network mesh, the plain text status could be CURLed from localhost:6782/status. The following status information was obtained from a worker node. We can check the number of connections between peers, or a number of peers, for example, from that URL:

```
$ curl localhost:6782/status
        Version: 2.1.3

        Service: router
       Protocol: weave 1..2
           Name: e6:cc:59:df:57:72(ip-172-31-11-209)
     Encryption: disabled
  PeerDiscovery: enabled
        Targets: 3
    Connections: 5 (5 established)
          Peers: 6 (with 30 established connections)
 TrustedSubnets: none

        Service: ipam
         Status: idle
          Range: 10.32.0.0/12
  DefaultSubnet: 10.32.0.0/12

        Service: plugin (v2)
```

The previous example shows us having six peers with five connections each. The IP range and the default subnet are important information for us to use when we create Docker networks. The IP range is 10.32.0.0/12, so if we create a network with subnet 10.32.0.0/24, it will be valid, while 10.0.0.0/24 will be invalid, for example.

The following figure illustrates our WeaveWorks network topology. Each node has five connections to another five nodes, as shown by solid lines from an **mg** node pointing to others. To make the diagram comprehensible, it shows only an **mg** node and another **wk** node connecting their five lines to the rest of the peers in the cluster:

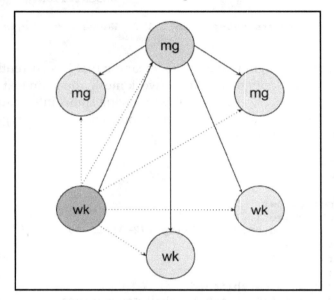

Figure 7.13: Swarm nodes connecting together via a WeaveWorks full-mesh network

For advanced troubleshooting, we could check the plugin's running process, `weaver`:

```
$ ps aux | grep weaver
root    4097   0.0 3.4 418660 34968 ? Ssl 06:15 0:06 /home/weave/weaver --
port=6783 --datapath=datapath --host-root=/host --proc-path=/host/proc --
http-addr=127.0.0.1:6784 --status-addr=0.0.0.0:6782 --no-dns --ipalloc-
range=10.32.0.0/12 --nickname ip-172-31-11-209 --log-level=debug --db-
prefix=/host/var/lib/weave/weave --plugin-v2 --plugin-mesh-socket= --
docker-api= 172.31.4.52 172.31.1.223 172.31.0.153
```

As you can see from grepping the output of `ps`, the final parts of the command are the list of Swarm manager IP addresses. If it looks like this, our networking layer is good to go. But if you do not see the list of manager IP addresses here, remove the plugin and start over again.

Creating a network

When we prepare a network with the WeaveWorks driver, please keep in mind that we always need to specify the `--subnet` and `--gateway` parameters as we do not use the default subnet value provided by the Docker's libnetwork. We need to make a network attachable, with `--attachable`, to allow containers started using `docker run` command attach to the network. Without this option, only Swarm services, started by `docker service create`, are allowed to join the network.

For example, we can create a *class C* network using the following command:

```
$ docker network create -d weaveworks/net-plugin:2.1.3 \
  --subnet=10.32.0.0/24 \
  --gateway=10.32.0.1 \
  --attachable my_net
```

Creating an operational control plane

An operational control plane is where we deploy operator containers to help operate the cluster. It is a concept that stems from the CoreOS's operator pattern, https://coreos.com/blog/operators.

Firstly, we create the control network to allow operator agents connecting to the manager nodes. Just name it `control`. We create this network to be a size of *class C*. So please be careful that the number of operator containers does not go beyond 255:

```
$ docker network create \
    --driver weaveworks/net-plugin:2.1.3 \
    --subnet 10.32.100.0/24 \
    --attachable \
    control
```

Operators in the `control` plane usually require access to Docker APIs to observe the cluster's state, to decide what to do, and to make changes back to the cluster.

To make the Docker API accessible via every operator inside the same control network, we deploy the `docker-api` service in the control plane.

We use `rancher/socat-docker` as the image of the `docker-api` service for the control plane because it is widely used and has proven stable for production. The `docker-api` will be deployed globally on every manager, using `node.role==manager`. The endpoint's mode will be set to `dnsrr` as each `docker-api` instance is stateless and the Docker managers are already taking care of the whole cluster state. So the `vip` endpoint mode is not necessary here.

Each `docker-api` instance binds to `/var/run/docker.sock` on their Docker host to connect to their local manager:

```
$ docker service create \
  --name=docker-api \
  --mode=global \
  --endpoint-mode=dnsrr \
  --network control \
  --constraint "node.role==manager" \
  --mount
"type=bind,source=/var/run/docker.sock,target=/var/run/docker.sock" \
  rancher/socat-docker
```

We will run an operator container called **service balancer** as an example of using the operator pattern in production.

Service balancer operator

Service rebalancing has been one of the requested features for Docker. However, it is better to have this feature running outside the orchestrator and to run it as an operator container.

The problem is that after a new node joins the cluster, we usually rebalance the running services to spread loads across the cluster. The main reason this feature is not built into the orchestrator is because it is application-specific. Also, if the cluster keeps rebalancing everything when nodes dynamically come and go, running services may be broken all the time, and not in a good enough condition to serve requests.

However, if we implement this kind of feature as an operator container, we can optionally disable it when necessary as it is running outside the orchestrator. Also, we can selectively pick only particular services to be rebalanced.

The service balancer is currently available as `chanwit/service-balancer` on Docker's hub. We will be running only one instance of service balancer on any manager:

```
$ docker service create \
  --name service-balancer \
  --network control \
  --constraint node.role==manager \
  --replicas 1 \
  chanwit/service-balancer
```

Something to consider when using the auto-rebalancer is that `--update-delay` must be set to greater than the startup time of each task. This is really important, especially for Java-based services. This delay should be large enough, at least larger than the interval used by the health checking mechanism.

Also, for the safest result, the value of `--update-parallelism` should start at 1, and gradually increase when the system can stably serve the requests.

To allow a service to automatically rebalance, the service balancer operator checks the service's label `rebalance.on.node.create=true`. If this label is present on the service, it will be rebalanced every time a new node is added to the cluster.

Logging

When it comes to logging, one popular solution is to set up an Elasticsearch stack. The natural combination could be **Elasticsearch-Logstash-Kibana (ELK)**.

We use an ELK stack from `https://github.com/deviantony/docker-elk` with modification to improve it by adding Docker Swarm configs, and to deploy each of them independently. The original Docker Compose file, `docker-compose.yml`, are split into three YML files, each for **Elasticsearch**, **Kibana**, and **Logstash**, respectively. Services must be deployed this way because we do not want to bring the whole logging system down when we change each service's configs. The fork used in this chapter is available at `https://github.com/chanwit/docker-elk`.

The following figure shows what the stack will look like. All ELK components will be in **elk_net**. The **Logstash** instance will be exposed on port **5000**. On each Docker host, its local **Logspout** agent will forward log messages from the Docker host to the **Logstash** instance. **Logstash** will then transform each message and store them in **ElasticSearch**. Finally, a user can access **Kibana** via port **5601** to visualize all the logs:

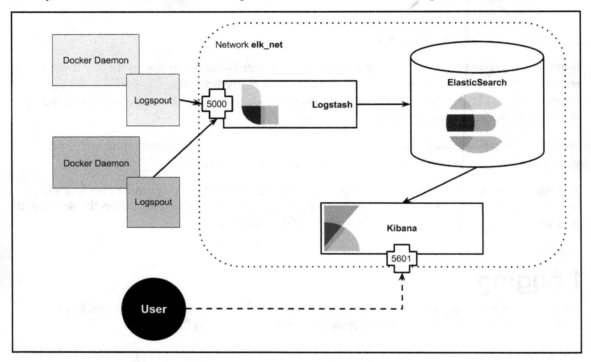

Figure 7.14: An ELK stack block diagram for cluster-wide logging

We start with the preparation of a dedicated network for our ELK stack. We name this network `elk_net` and use it for all ELK components:

```
docker network create \
  --driver weaveworks/net-plugin:2.1.3 \
  --subnet 10.32.200.0/24 \
  --attachable \
  elk_net
```

The following is the source of `elasticsearch.yml`. We use Docker compose YAML specification version 3.3 throughout the chapter. This is the minimum requirement, as we will use Docker Swarm configs to manage all configuration files for us:

```
version: '3.3'

configs:
  elasticsearch_config:
    file: ./elasticsearch/config/elasticsearch.yml

services:
  elasticsearch:
    build:
      context: elasticsearch/
    image: chanwit/elasticsearch:6.1
    configs:
      - source: elasticsearch_config
        target: /usr/share/elasticsearch/config/elasticsearch.yml
    environment:
      ES_JAVA_OPTS: "-Xmx512m -Xms512m"

networks:
  default:
    external:
      name: elk_net
```

It is the requirement that `docker stack` needs the image name to be specified before it can be deployed. So, we need to build the container image using `docker-compose` first.

 We use `docker-compose` only for building images.

Let's do it! We use `docker-compose` build to prepare images defined in the YML file. The `docker-compose` command also tags images for us too. As we have a separate YML file each service, we use `-f` to tell `docker-compose` to build the correct file:

```
$ docker-compose -f elasticsearch.yml build
```

When the image is ready, we can simply deploy the stack, `es`, using the following command:

```
$ docker stack deploy -c elasticsearch.yml es
```

Next, we move to the preparation and deployment of Kibana.

Here's the stack YML file for Kibana. We have `kibana_config` pointing to our Kibana configuration. The Kibana port `5601` is published using Swarm's host mode to bypass the ingress layer. Please remember that we do not really have the default ingress layer in our cluster. As previously mentioned, we use Træfik as our new ingress:

```
version: '3.3'

configs:
  kibana_config:
    file: ./kibana/config/kibana.yml

services:
  kibana:
    build:
      context: kibana/
    image: chanwit/kibana:6.1
    configs:
      - source: kibana_config
        target: /usr/share/kibana/config/kibana.yml
    ports:
      - published: 5601
        target: 5601
        mode: host

networks:
  default:
    external:
      name: elk_net
```

Similar to Elasticsearch, now the Kibana image can be prepared using the `docker-compose build` command:

```
$ docker-compose -f kibana.yml build
```

After that, we deploy Kibana with the stack name `kb`:

```
$ docker stack deploy -c kibana.yml kb
```

With Logstash, there are two configuration files to consider. The most important one is the pipeline config, `logstash_pipeline_config`. We need to add custom rules to this file for log message transformation. It keeps changing, unlike the first two components of ELK. Logstash listens to port `5000`, both for TCP and UDP, inside `elk_net`. We will later plug Logspout into this network to convey log messages from Docker daemons to this Logstash service:

```
version: '3.3'

configs:
  logstash_config:
    file: ./logstash/config/logstash.yml
  logstash_pipeline_config:
    file: ./logstash/pipeline/logstash.conf

services:
  logstash:
    build:
      context: logstash/
    image: chanwit/logstash:6.1
    configs:
      - source: logstash_config
        target: /usr/share/logstash/config/logstash.yml
      - source: logstash_pipeline_config
        target: /usr/share/logstash/pipeline/logstash.conf
    environment:
      LS_JAVA_OPTS: "-Xmx256m -Xms256m"

networks:
  default:
    external:
      name: elk_net
```

The next steps are to build and deploy, similar to the first two components:

```
$ docker-compose -f logstash.yml build
$ docker stack deploy -c logstash.yml log
```

We started these three components as separate stacks linked together via `elk_net`. To check if all components are running, simply check this using `docker stack ls`:

```
$ docker stack ls
NAME      SERVICES
es        1
kb        1
log       1
```

Finally, we can redirect all logs from each Docker daemon to the ELK stack, the central service, using Logspout. This can be done by attaching each local `logspout` container to the `elk_net` so that they will all be able to connect to a Logstash instance inside the network. We start each Logspout using the following command:

```
$ docker run -d \
  --name=logspout \
  --network=elk_net \
  --volume=/var/run/docker.sock:/var/run/docker.sock \
  gliderlabs/logspout \
  syslog+tcp+udp://logstash:5000
```

We are now able to log all messages via Logspout to Logstash, storing them in Elasticsearch, and visualizing them with Kibana.

Scripting Docker with Golang

When it comes to operating and administrating Docker, we could do everything by controlling the cluster via the `docker` CLI using the `jq` command. Another powerful and very flexible way is to control the cluster via scripting. The most suitable programming language for scripting Docker cluster is, of course, Golang.

Why not Python? How could Golang, a statically compiled language, come to fit scripting?

- First, Go is the language that Docker is written in. The Docker library written in the Go language is the same piece of codes used by Docker itself. So, the scripts written using this library will be naturally in high quality and greatly reliable.
- Second, the language constructs and the idioms fit the way Docker works. For example, the Go programming language has the channel construct and it fits nicely for processing event messages emitted by the Docker cluster.
- Third, the Go compiler is incredibly fast. Also, once all related libraries get compiled, the compilation time is greatly reduced. We can normally use it to run scripts just like other scripting language interpreters.

In this section, we will discuss how to use scripts written in Golang to control Docker directly via its API. This will become a powerful tool for taking care of running the cluster.

Preparing the tool

Installing the Go compiler and making it ready to use is sometimes tricky. However, **Golang Version Manager** (**GVM**), is a tool that helps with installing and uninstalling different Go versions on the same machine. It also helps manage GOPATH effectively.

What is GOPATH? It is defined as follows in Wikipedia:

> *"The GOPATH environment variable is used to specify directories outside of $GOROOT that contain the source for Go projects and their binaries."*

To start using GVM, we first install the gvm command using the snippet provided on https://github.com/moovweb/gvm. It can be installed with a single command:

```
$ bash < <(curl -s -S -L
https://raw.githubusercontent.com/moovweb/gvm/master/binscripts/gvm-install
er)
```

Now we have GVM installed already, and we continue by installing Go.

It is great to use Go's most recent version-1.9.3. The command to install is, of course, gvm install. We pass the -B parameter to the install command, so that it will download and use only the binary of the Go distribution:

```
$ gvm install go1.9.3 -B
Installing go1.9.3 from binary source
```

Next, if we choose to go with Go v1.9.3 when taking care of our cluster, we should make it the default version. Issue the gvm use command with the --default parameter to do so:

```
$ gvm use go1.9.3 --default
Now using version go1.9.3
```

Making Go scriptable

Next, prepare the next tool, gorun, to make a Go program scriptable. With gorun, you can add a shebang to the first line of the script, as shown in the following command:

```
#!/usr/bin/env gorun
```

The normal Go program will then be allowed to execute directly from the shell.

To install `gorun`, just do `go get`. The `gorun` binary will now be available under the path provided by the current `go1.9.3` managed by GVM. Please note that if you switch Go version with GVM, you need to do `go get` again:

```
$ go get github.com/erning/gorun
```

We could install all necessary libraries for controlling Docker programmatically by installing the Docker client library itself:

```
$ go get github.com/docker/docker/client
```

If nothing goes wrong, we will be ready to start writing a Golang script.

Simple Docker script

Let's write a simple script that interacts with Docker:

```
#!/usr/bin/env gorun
package main

import (
  "fmt"
  "context"

  "github.com/docker/docker/client"
)

func main() {
  ctx := context.Background()

  cli, err := client.NewClient(client.DefaultDockerHost, "1.30", nil, nil)
  if err != nil {
    panic(err)
  }

  info, err := cli.Info(ctx)
  if err != nil {
    panic(err)
  }

  fmt.Println(info.ServerVersion)
}
```

First, the script must have the first line with shebang and `gorun`. Second, import a line with Docker's client library, `github.com/docker/docker/client`. Although, Docker has been moved to `github.com/moby/moby`, but we still need to import all related library using the `docker/docker` repository name. Just `go get github.com/docker/docker/client` and everything is still working fine for us.

Then we start programming our cluster by creating a client while also setting the API version to 1.30. This script then calls `cli.Info(ctx)` to obtain the engine's information from the Docker daemon, as the `info` variable. It simply prints out the version of the Docker daemon we're talking to. The version information is stored in `info.ServerVersion`.

Save the script to a file named `server-version`. We can now run it as a normal shell script:

```
$ chmod +x ./server-version
$ ./server-version
17.06.2-ce
```

Script reacting to Docker events

Next, we will write a script to monitor changes in the Docker cluster and then do a print out when a node is updated:

```
#!/usr/bin/env gorun
package main

import (
  "context"
  "fmt"

  "github.com/docker/docker/api/types"
  "github.com/docker/docker/api/types/filters"
  "github.com/docker/docker/client"
)

func main() {
  ctx := context.Background()

  cli, err := client.NewClient(client.DefaultDockerHost, "1.30", nil, nil)
  if err != nil {
    panic(err)
  }
```

```
filter := filters.NewArgs(filters.Arg("type", "node"))
ch, _ := cli.Events(ctx, types.EventsOptions{
  Filters: filter,
})

for {

  fmt.Println("Waiting for event ...")
  message := <-ch
  action := message.Action

  switch action {
  case "create":
    fmt.Println(" - New node added.")
  case "update":
    fmt.Println(" - Node updated.")
  case "remove":
    fmt.Println(" - Node removed.")
  }

}

}
```

This is also a script executed by `gorun`. The script starts by creating a Docker client CLI pointing to the local socket, `/var/run/docker.sock`.

Then it creates a filter, the `filter` variable. This filter makes the event emitter select only the type of events we are interested in, in this case, when the `type` of events is `node`. This is equivalent to passing `--filter type=node` to the command line.
The `cli.Events` method will return a Go channel for retrieving messages. A message is then retrieved inside the `for` loop. The program will be automatically blocked if the message is not available in the channel. So the script just becomes a single-thread style and easy to program.

Inside the loop, we can manipulate information inside the message, for example, checking the action of a certain event. Normally, most types of event contain three possible actions, create, update, and remove. For a node, create means there is a new node added to the cluster. The update action means something has changed on a certain node. The remove action means the node is removed from the cluster.

Just save this script to ./node-event, then chmod +x it.

```
$ chmod +x ./node-event
```

 The chmod command will change executable bits of the script. With these bits, the Linux system will be able to detect that the file should be executed. Then, it will tell gorun to take care of that execution.

Try changing some properties of the current working node. We may observe that the text – Node updated. will be printed out.

Exercises

Please try to answer the following questions without going back to read the chapter's content:

1. List at least three components described in the stable cluster configuration.
2. Why are retry and circuit breaker important?
3. How do we replace the default ingress layer with the new one?
4. How can we install the network plugin?
5. What is the most frontal part of the ELK stack?
6. Why is the Go language suitable for scripting the Docker system?
7. How do we listen to Docker events of a certain type?
8. How do we set up a control plane?
9. What is the operator pattern? Why is it important?
10. What is the characteristic of Spot instances that makes them cheaper than normal instances?

Summary

This chapter discussed various topics on how to prepare and operate a Docker cluster with a stable configuration. We introduced a low-cost alternative to Lambda by deploying a Docker cluster on Spot instances. This chapter also introduced the concept of CoreOS's operator pattern, and how to use it practically to auto-balance the tasks of our cluster.

When it comes to logging, the ELK stack is usually the first choice. This chapter also discussed how to efficiently prepare ELK on Docker Swarm and it ended with how to operate a cluster with Golang scripts, the scripting technique that can fully leverage Docker and its ecosystem.

In the next chapter, we will put all FaaS platforms into the same cluster and make them work together to demonstrate a use case of event-driven FaaS systems over a Docker cluster.

Putting Them All Together

8

In this chapter, we will walk through an example to demonstrate serverless platforms working together on a Docker cluster, and we will demonstrate several serverless/FaaS use cases.

We will discuss a mobile payment scenario and implement it using functions but, unusually at this level of infrastructure, we will connect all three FaaS platforms together. The main ideas demonstrated by the content of this chapter are the concept of using functions as a **Glue**, using functions to wrap the legacy web-based application, and using functions as a data stream processing program.

In the next section, we will start with the settings and scenario used by this chapter.

The topics covered in this chapter are:

- A mobile payment scenario
- A Parse platform as a backend
- Preparing a WebHook in Fn
- An event state machine with a blockchain
- Wrapping a legacy with a function
- Using a function as a Glue
- A stream processor
- Inter-FaaS platform networking

A mobile payment scenario

We are using a mobile payment with a money transfer allowed between two banks as the scenario for this chapter. With the money transfer, the business logic is easy to understand. So, we do not need to worry about this part. Let's focus on the complexity of the architecture.

Money transfer between two different banks with different underlying implementations is hard. This is because we cannot directly apply the *concept of traditional transactions* to cope with external systems. The system is presented in the following diagram:

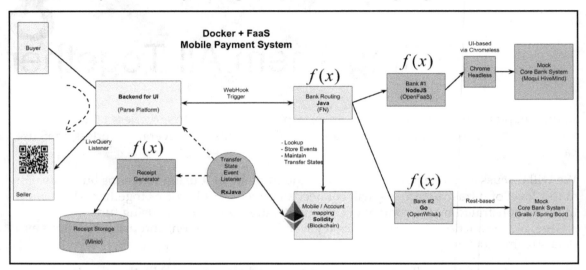

Figure 8.1: The overall block diagram of the mobile payment system

What are we not covering in this chapter?

The UI parts are out beyond scope of this book, so they are not available. The **Receipt Generator** and the **Receipt Storage** are optional. They are left for you to implement, if interested.

What do we implement and demonstrate? Let's discuss:

- The Parse platform, as a backend for the UI.
- The **Bank Routing** function. It is written in Java and deployed on Fn. This component is called `routing_fn`.
- **Bank #1** and its function calling to a legacy web-based system. The function here is written in Node.js using the `chromeless` library (https://github.com/graphcool/chromeless). The function connects to a headless Chrome instance, our familiar web browser. The function drives Chrome to navigate and create a transaction for us on a real ERP system. We use Moqui as our ERP backend. Actually, Moqui comes with a complete set of REST APIs, but we intentionally use its web base to simulate the scenario where we need to modernize some legacy systems. The function of this part is called `hivectl`.

- **Bank #2** and its function, `account_ctl`, connecting to a REST-based bank system. The function is written using `Go` and will be running on OpenWhisk. The mock bank server behind this component is a simple one written using the Grails/Spring Boot framework. We use this component to demonstrate how to write a FaaS function to wrap and simplify a REST-based API. The **Bank Routing** function, `routing_fn`, will be selectively called by each bank. This **Bank #2** component will be used together with **Bank #1** there.

- A set of smart contracts written in **Solidity** to maintain the mapping of mobile numbers to bank accounts. Also, another set of smart contracts will be used to maintain the state of the money transfer of each transaction.

- An agent written in Java and the RxJava library to demonstrate a data stream processing component that calls a function and diverts the event to other parts of the system.

A Parse platform as a backend

What is Parse? Similar to Firebase, Parse is a **Backend as a Service (BaaS)** platform. With Parse, developers do not need to code the backend system themselves for their UIs or mobile applications. Parse is used by mobile application developers to help accelerate the development process. Together with the Parse dashboard, they provide an easy UI to craft all data entities, called *classes*, needed to process basic business logic.

Preparation

Here's how to create a Docker network and deploy a set of Docker compose files. We use the concept of metastack to deploy multiple stacks and have some labels and naming conventions to group them together:

```
$ docker network create \
  --driver=weaveworks/net-plugin:2.1.3 \
  --subnet=10.32.2.0/24 \
  --attachable \
  parse_net

$ docker volume create mongo_data

$ docker stack deploy -c mongodb.yml          parse_01
$ docker stack deploy -c parse.yml            parse_02
$ docker stack deploy -c parse_dashboard.yml  parse_03
$ docker stack deploy -c ingress.yml          parse_04
```

While deploying things on production, we do not set up the network and volumes with any Docker compose files. All stacks should refer to external volumes and networks.

Starting with MongoDB, we have already set up a volume for it. The following is the setup of the MongoDB server:

```
version: '3.3'

services:
  mongo:
    image: mongo:3.6.1-jessie
    volumes:
      - mongo_data:/data/db

volumes:
  mongo_data:
    external: true

networks:
  default:
    external:
      name: parse_net
```

We move to the next component, the Parse platform. To make the container work with Træfik, we put some labels to the service, saying that it will be on the `parse_net` network and will expose port `1337` to Træfik's ingress.

We add a rule to allow every HTTP method, also to define the custom entrypoint, and allow `Origin=*` to enable the Parse dashboard, the next section, to be able to connect to the Parse server:

```
version: '3.3'

services:

  parse_server:
    image: parseplatform/parse-server:2.6.5
    command: --appId APP1 --masterKey MASTER_KEY --databaseURI
mongodb://mongo/prod
    deploy:
      labels:
        - "traefik.docker.network=parse_net"
        - "traefik.port=1337"
        - "traefik.frontend.rule=Method:
GET,POST,PUT,DELETE,OPTIONS,HEAD,CONNECT"
        - "traefik.frontend.entryPoints=parse_server"
```

```
        - "traefik.frontend.headers.customresponseheaders.Access-Control-
Allow-Origin=*"

networks:
  default:
    external:
      name: parse_net
```

Here's the Parse dashboard and its configuration. The current version of the dashboard is 1.1.2. It will be exposed to port 4040 via Træfik's ingress:

```
version: '3.3'

services:

  parse_dashboard:
    image: parseplatform/parse-dashboard:1.1.2
    environment:
      - PARSE_DASHBOARD_ALLOW_INSECURE_HTTP=true
    deploy:
      labels:
        - "traefik.docker.network=parse_net"
        - "traefik.port=4040"
        - "traefik.frontend.rule=Method:
GET,POST,PUT,DELETE,OPTIONS,HEAD,CONNECT"
        - "traefik.frontend.entryPoints=parse_dashboard"
        - "traefik.frontend.headers.customresponseheaders.Access-Control-
Allow-Origin=*"
      configs:
        - source: config.json
          target: /src/Parse-Dashboard/parse-dashboard-config.json

configs:
  config.json:
    file: ./config.json

networks:
  default:
    external:
      name: parse_net
```

The configuration defines the default username and password, and also says that the server allows a connection via HTTP. Setting INSECURE to be true is fine, as we could do SSL simply at the ingress layer, using Træfik:

```
{
  "apps": [
    {
      "serverURL": "http://localhost:1337/parse",
      "appId": "APP1",
      "masterKey": "MASTER_KEY",
      "appName": "APP1",
      "iconName": "MyAppIcon.png",
      "supportedPushLocales": ["en", "ru", "fr"]
    }
  ],
  "users": [
    {
      "user":"admin",
      "pass":"password"
    }
  ],
  "iconsFolder": "icons",
  "allowInsecureHTTP": true
}
```

The following YAML code is to define the L7 Træfik ingress for Parse and Parse dashboard. We have to expose Parse to the outside too, as the dashboard is a fat client, rather than server-side rendering. This is the main reason we need to set Allow-Origin=*:

```
version: '3.3'

services:

  l7:
    image: traefik:1.5.2
    command: --docker
      --docker.swarmmode
      --docker.watch
      --docker.endpoint=tcp://docker-api:2375
      --entryPoints="Name:parse_server Address::1337"
      --entryPoints="Name:parse_dashboard Address::4040"
      --web --logLevel=DEBUG
    ports:
      - published: 1337
        target: 1337
        protocol: tcp
        mode: host
```

```
      - published: 4040
        target: 4040
        protocol: tcp
        mode: host

  networks:
    default:
      external:
        name: parse_net
```

If everything goes well, we can open our favorite browser and navigate to `localhost:4040` for the Parse dashboard, as shown in the following screenshot. The default **Username** and **Password** are: `admin/password`:

Figure 8.2: The login page of the Parse dashboard

Here, in the following screenshot, the dashboard of our Parse platform **APP1** connects to the Parse instance at `http://localhost:1337`:

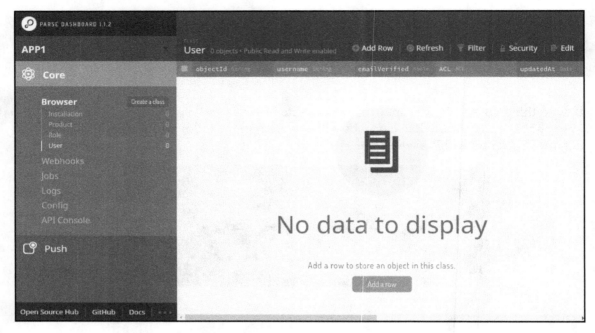

Figure 8.3: The Parse application screen showing the core part

Defining a transfer entity

On the left-hand side navigation pane, we see the **Core** | **Browser** menu. This is where we can see all the data on our Parse platform. There are already some built-in classes, but we are going to define a new class to help do the money transfer.

Click on **Create a class** in the **Core** | **Browser** menu. A dialog box, as shown in the following screenshot, will appear. We will use it to name our new class, `Transfer`. This will be our main entity responsible for mobile payment and, of course, money transfer:

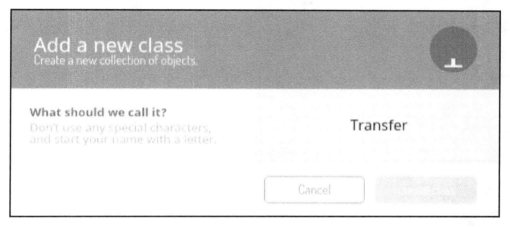

Figure 8.4: A dialog for defining a new class in Parse

Then we need to set up some new columns for this entity. We define the following columns:

- **from**: The mobile number to pay money.
- **to**: The mobile number to receive money.
- **amount**: The amount of money to pay.
- **sent**: A flag needs to be set to `true` when we want to start to process the transaction. If this field is `null` or `false`, the WebHook (see next) will just receive data and do nothing.
- **processed**: A flag will be automatically set to `true` if the transaction is finished processing.

How can we use this class? Using the dashboard, as shown in the following screenshot, we set mobile numbers for the **from, to,** and **amount** columns. Then, when we are ready, just set the **sent** column to `true`.

If the processing goes wrong, the **sent** flag will be reset to `null` automatically by the WebHook:

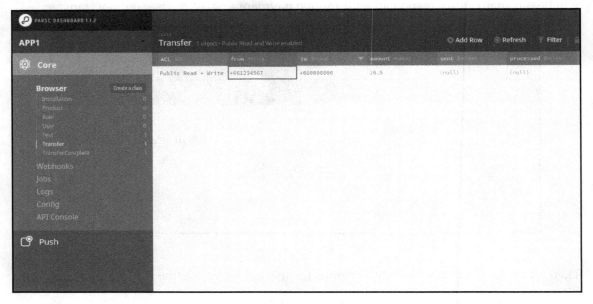

Figure 8.5: Browsing the Transfer class using the dashboard

WebHook

The Parse platform provides an extensible mechanism to allow us to process business logic externally. This is where functions come in. This mechanism is called **WebHook**.

We may have functions running as external processes, outside the Parse platform, and use them in conjunction with Parse's WebHook to perform complex business logic. As in the previous example, we already have the `Transfer` class. We then define a WebHook for this class to call an external function every time, before each of the `Transfer` entities is saved. We specify a URL to a FaaS gateway for this WebHook. The `HTTP POST` method will be made to the specified URL with the JSON as its request body. The request body contains the data of the current `Transfer` entity.

A WebHook in Parse can be created by going to **Core** | **Webhooks** and clicking on the small **Create a webhook** option:

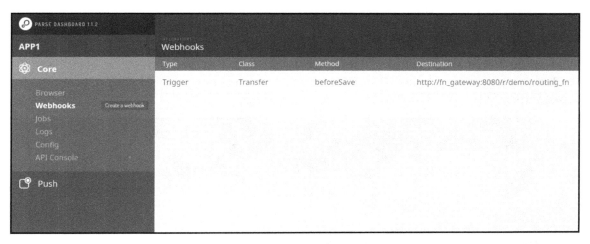

Figure 8.6: A screen for listing the existing WebHooks

There are two kinds of WebHook in Parse: Cloud Code functions and triggers. The kind we are using in this chapter is the **trigger**. A WebHook trigger can hook into many places, such as **beforeSave**, **afterSave**, **beforeDelete**, and **afterDelete**.

In the example we are discussing in this chapter, the **beforeSave** trigger will be used as shown in the following screenshot. We choose **Transfer** as the target class of this hook. Then we need to specify the **Webhook URL**, a bank routing function deployed to Fn:

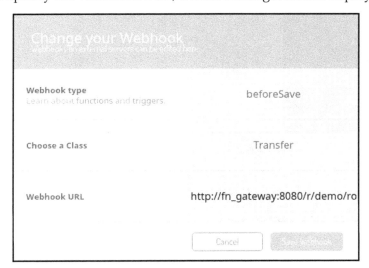

Figure 8.7: A dialog for defining a new WebHook; beforeSave for class Transfer

We will talk about the bank routing WebHook in the next section, but let's see it in action briefly before we explore its details.

We test the WebHook by sending data by creating a new instance of the `Transfer` class. In the following screenshot, mobile number `+661234567` is not registered yet. So it cannot be looked up, and the WebHook returns an error message:

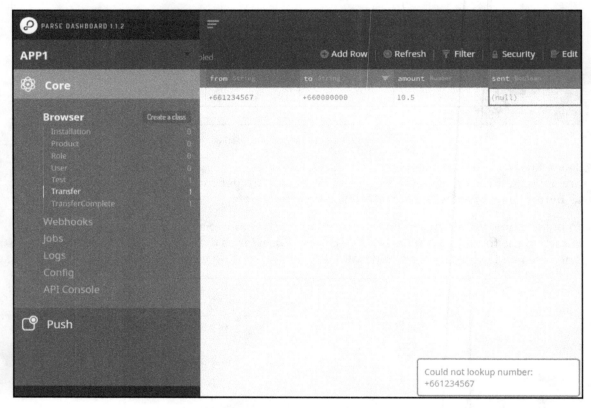

Figure 8.8: An error message sent back from the WebHook will pop up on the bottom right

To see error logs, click on **Core | Logs,** as shown in the following screenshot. Here is an example of the Webhook returning the following JSON:

```
{"error": "Could not lookup number: +661234567"}
```

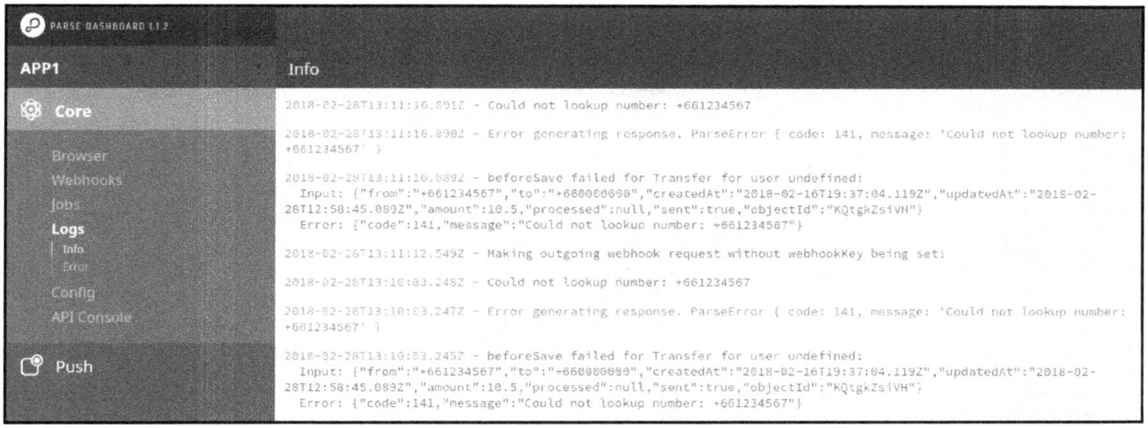

Figure 8.9: Info-level log screen displaying all kind of logs, including errors

The specifications of the returning messages are `{"success": object}` to update data back to the Parse platform, and `{"error":"msg"}` to display the error message.

Preparing a WebHook in Fn

The Fn Project works best with functions written in Java. When calling a function, the framework would be able to automatically transform the body of the request as a parameter of the entrypoint method. In the following example, the JSON from the request will be converted into a string for the `handleRequest` method, the entrypoint method of this Fn function:

```java
public Object handleRequest(String body) {
    if (body == null || body.isEmpty()) {
        body = "{}";
    }
    Input input;
    try {
        val mapper = new ObjectMapper();
        input = mapper.readValue(body, Input.class);
    } catch (IOException e) {
        return new Error(e.getMessage());
    }
    if (input == null) {
        return new Error(body);
    }
    /* process the rest of business logic */
}
```

Here's the list of **data transfer object (DTO)** classes to properly encode and decode Parse's WebHook messages inside an Fn function. With help from Project Lombok and Jackson, we can dramatically reduce numbers of lines of code. An `Input` object is the wrapper for a Java's `Transfer` object, that contains all columns similar to the `Transfer` class, which we have defined on the Parse platform.

 Please note that we have a **Transfer** class on both sides of the system, on the Parse platform, and also on the Fn platform.

The `Success` and `Error` class are for returning processing results back to Parse:

```
@Data
@AllArgsConstructor
@JsonIgnoreProperties(ignoreUnknown = true)
public static class Input {
    private Transfer object;
}

@Data
@NoArgsConstructor
@JsonIgnoreProperties(ignoreUnknown = true)
public static class Transfer {
    private String objectId;
    private String from;
    private String to;
    private Double amount;
    private Boolean sent;
    private Boolean processed;
}

@Data
@AllArgsConstructor
public static class Success {
    private Transfer success;
}

@Data
@AllArgsConstructor
public static class Error {
    private String error;
}
```

As it is a Java project, we do not need to build it inside the container. Here's the Gradle build file, which could be built using the `gradle installDist` command:

```
plugins {
    id 'io.franzbecker.gradle-lombok' version '1.11'
    id 'java'
    id 'groovy'
    id 'application'
}

mainClassName = 'App'

dependencies {
    // FN Project
    compile 'com.fnproject.fn:api:1.0.56'

    // JSON encoding
    compile 'com.fasterxml.jackson.core:jackson-annotations:2.9.4'
    compile 'com.fasterxml.jackson.core:jackson-databind:2.9.4'

    // REST client
    compile 'com.squareup.okhttp3:okhttp:3.9.1'

    // Simplify Java syntax
    compile group: 'org.projectlombok', name: 'lombok-maven',
            version: '1.16.20.0', ext: 'pom'

    // Ethereum Client
    compile 'org.web3j:core:3.2.0'

    // Testing
    testCompile 'com.fnproject.fn:testing:1.0.56'
    testCompile 'junit:junit:4.12'
    testCompile 'org.codehaus.groovy:groovy-all:2.4.12'
    testCompile 'org.spockframework:spock-core:1.0-groovy-2.4'
}

repositories {
    mavenCentral()
    jcenter()
    maven {
        url "https://dl.bintray.com/fnproject/fnproject"
    }
}
```

The following is the Dockerfile to build an image for the Fn Project. It needs to inherit from `fn-java-fdk`. We use `jdk9-1.0.56` for the demo in this book. What you do is copy all JAR files from the `build` directory to the `/function/app` inside the container image:

```
FROM fnproject/fn-java-fdk:jdk9-1.0.56

WORKDIR /function

COPY ./build/install/routing_fn/lib/*.jar /function/app/

CMD ["com.example.fn.TransferFunction::handleRequest"]
```

The following steps are to prepare the Fn server, and then we build our function with the `gradle` command. Then we build and push its Docker image onto the hub before redefining it as an Fn route.

First, we deploy an Fn Server manually with the following `docker run` command. Also, we attach Fn to the `parse_net`. There is a special hack to Fn so that we can make every container started by Fn be in the same network, as specified by `FN_NETWORK` there:

```
docker run \
  --name fnserver \
  --detach \
  -v /var/run/docker.sock:/var/run/docker.sock \
  -v fn_vol:/app/data \
  -p 28080:8080 \
  --network=parse_net \
  --network-alias=fn_gateway \
  -e FN_LOG_LEVEL=debug \
  -e FN_NETWORK=parse_net \
  fnproject/fnserver
```

Here's the build and push script. Save the following scripts as `./buildAndPush`:

```
./gradlew installDist

VERSION=$1

docker build -t chanwit/routing_fn:$VERSION .
docker push chanwit/routing_fn:$VERSION

fn routes delete demo /routing_fn
fn routes create /routing_fn -i chanwit/routing_fn:$VERSION demo
```

Then we can start the build and push process by calling the script with a certain version number, as in the following:

```
./buildAndPush v1
```

In the next section, we will discuss how the WebHook function looks up account data from a blockchain and how we can track the states of each money transfer transaction.

An event state machine with a blockchain

We use an *Ethereum blockchain* as the event state machine for the money transfer system. A blockchain in this role is used for storing the following:

- The mapping between telephone numbers and bank accounts
- The overall state of each transfer transaction

Inside the blockchain, there are two kinds of smart contracts. The first one implements the **repository pattern**, and the second one implements the **entity model**.

We use Truffle (`http://truffleframework.com/`) to create this event state machine. Look at the subproject named *eventmachine* in the GitHub repository (`https://github.com/chanwit/eventmachine`).

Here's a smart contract under the `entities/` directory, `TransferState.sol`. This smart contract maintains the states of each transfer transaction. Each transaction is initialized with **NONE**, then **STARTED**, **PENDING**, and finally **COMPLETED**. The following diagram illustrates the smart contract `TransferState` working together with its repository implementation:

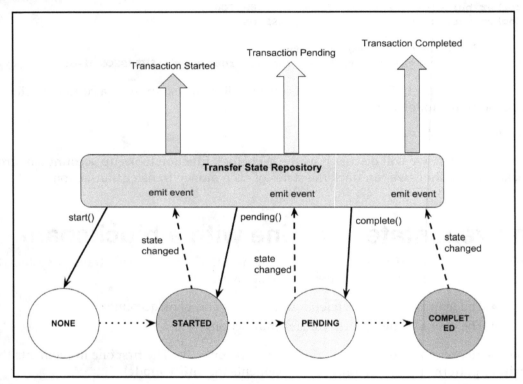

Figure 8.10: Flow of state transition and event emission by smart contracts

We then explore its code for a bit. When moving to the next state, we use the `require` statement to check and let the smart contract throw an exception, if the pre-condition is not met:

```
contract TransferState {

    enum State { NONE, STARTED, PENDING, COMPLETED }

    string txId;
    State state;

    function TransferState(string _txId) {
```

```
    state = State.NONE;
    txId = _txId;
  }

  function start() public {
    require(state == State.NONE);
    state = State.STARTED;
  }

  function pending() public {
    require(state == State.STARTED);
    state = State.PENDING;
  }

  function complete() public {
    require(state == State.PENDING);
    state = State.COMPLETED;
  }

  function currentState() public constant returns (uint8) {
    return uint8(state);
  }
}
```

As previously mentioned, the `TransferState` is managed by the smart contract `TransferStateRepository`. Basically, this is an implementation of the repository pattern (`https://hub.packtpub.com/domain-driven-design/`). Additionally, this smart contract naturally runs on the blockchain. To allow it to communicate with the outside world, every smart contract has to emit a kind of event. In the case of this `TransferStateRepository`, it has been designed to emit events when each transaction changes its status to `STARTED`, `PENDING`, and also `COMPLETED`. See the event signatures there in *Figure 8.10*:

```
contract TransferStateRepository {

    event TransferStarted(string txId);
    event TransferPending(string txId);
    event TransferCompleted(string txId);

    mapping(bytes32 => address) states;

    function start(string txId) public {
        /* register the state, set to STARTED */
        TransferStarted(txId);
    }
```

```
function pending(string txId) public {
    /* check the state, set to PENDING */
    TransferPending(txId);
}

function complete(string txId) public {
    /* check the state, set to COMPLETED */
    TransferCompleted(txId);
}

function getStateOf(string txId) public constant returns (string) {
    /**/
    if (state == 0) return "NONE";
    else if (state == 1) return "STARTED";
    else if (state == 2) return "PENDING";
    else if (state == 3) return "COMPLETED";
}
}
```

The mapping between telephone numbers and bank accounts is maintained by RegistrationRepository. This smart contract uses the same technique to communicate with the outside world, emitting events.

There are four events designed for RegistrationRepository. The Registered event is fired when we register a new telephone number into the mapping. If we try to register the same number again, the AlreadyExisted event is fired from the blockchain.

RegistrationFound is the event fired when we find a mobile number by name via the findTelByNo function and when this function cannot find any registration matched by the input mobile number, the RegistrationNotFound event is emitted:

```
contract RegistrationRepository {

    mapping(bytes32 => address) registrations;

    event Registered(string telNo, address registration);
    event AlreadyExisted(string telNo);
    event RegistrationFound(string telNo, string bank, string accNo);
    event RegistrationNotFound(string telNo);

    function register(string telNo, string bank, string accNo) public {
        /**/
        Registered(telNo, address(r));
    }

    function findByTelNo(string telNo) public returns (address) {
```

```
/**/
Registration r = Registration(registrations[key]);
RegistrationFound(telNo, to_s(r.bank()), to_s(r.accNo()));

return address(r);
    }

}
```

Using the Truffle framework, we are allowed to initialize some data with JavaScript during the development. Here's one of the migration scripts, found under the `migrations/` directory, that is used for deploying smart contracts to the blockchain and registering two mobile numbers. The first number links to an account managed by an account managed by **Bank #1**, the OpenFaaS bank. The second mobile number is registered and linked to **Bank #2**, the OpenWhisk bank. In all banks, we already have accounts containing deposits:

```
var RegistrationRepository = artifacts.require(
  "./v2/repository/RegistrationRepository.sol");
var TransferStateRepository = artifacts.require(
  "./v2/repository/TransferStateRepository.sol");

module.exports = function(deployer) {

  deployer.deploy(TransferStateRepository);

  deployer.deploy(RegistrationRepository).then(function() {
    RegistrationRepository.deployed().then(function(repo){
      repo.register("+661234567", "faas", "55700").then();
      repo.register("+661111111", "whisk", "A1234").then();
    });
  });

};
```

We set up an Ethereum blockchain network with Parity, one of the most stable Ethereum clients. Here's the setup. We attach the running Parity container to the same network of both Fn and the Parse platform:

```
docker run --rm --name=parity_dev -d -p 8545:8545 -p 8180:8180 \
    --network=parse_net \
    --network-alias=blockchain \
    parity/parity:stable-release \
    --geth --chain dev --force-ui \
    --reseal-min-period 0 \
    --jsonrpc-cors http://localhost \
```

```
--jsonrpc-apis all \
--jsonrpc-interface 0.0.0.0 \
--jsonrpc-hosts all
```

For the production private blockchain network, we need to set things up differently. For example, we need to set up our own genesis block and the mining behavior of the network. Anyway, it is beyond the scope of this book. We then deploy the smart contract via Truffle:

```
$ cd eventmachine
$ truffle exec scripts/unlock.js
$ truffle migrate
```

How the WebHook uses the blockchain

We will regularly go back to the WebHook after discussing each component around it.

We already know how our blockchain and smart contracts work. They record mobile number registration, and maintain states of transfer transactions. In this section, we discuss how the WebHook function interacts with the blockchain. The following is the snippet from the WebHook function. The lookup method inside the function obtains the smart contract `RegistrationRepository` and then invokes `findByTelNo()` on the blockchain. The result is then available inside a transaction receipt. We check what kind of event is stored inside that receipt. If it is an `RegistrationFound` event, then this method returns a result object containing information regarding the bank name and account number.

There is room for improving this check.

How should the reader optimize the smart contract to fire only one event and meaningfully check whether the telephone number is already registered or not?

That is basically about the lookup part:

```
@Data
@AllArgsConstructor
static class RegistrationResult {
    private String bankName;
    private String accountId;
}

public RegistrationResult lookup(String telNo) throws Exception {
    val repo = ContractRegistry.registrationRepository();
    val receipt = repo.findByTelNo(telNo).send();
    val foundEvents = repo.getRegistrationFoundEvents(receipt);
```

```
    if (foundEvents.isEmpty() == false) {
        val reg = foundEvents.get(0);
        return new RegistrationResult(reg.bank, reg.accNo);
    } else {
        val notFoundEvents = repo.getRegistrationNotFoundEvents(receipt);
        if(notFoundEvents.isEmpty() == false) {
            val reg = notFoundEvents.get(0);
            return null;
        }
    }

    throw new Exception("Lookup does not find any event in receipt.");
}
```

The transfer state management part is implemented inside a set of methods whose names start with `transfer`.

Here's the method to tell that we start new transactions with ID `txId`. It uses the `ContractRegistry` to obtain the smart contract, `TransferStateRepository`. Then we create a new transaction state and set its state to be `STARTED`. If everything is OK, we should get a transaction receipt from the call with an event, `TransferStartedEvent`, embedded in the receipt:

```
private boolean transferStart(String txId) {
    try {
        val repo = ContractRegistry.transferStateRepository();
        val receipt = repo.start(txId).send();
        val events = repo.getTransferStartedEvents(receipt);
        if (events.isEmpty()) {
            return false;
        }
        return true;
    } catch (Exception e) {
        return false;
    }
}
```

Wrapping a legacy with a function

In this section, we will demonstrate how to write a wrapper function for a legacy web-based system. To achieve this, we use the `chromeless` library (https://github.com/graphcool/chromeless) to connect to a headless Chrome instance. Then the `chromeless` script drives the Chrome browser to do the rest for us.

The following diagram shows the working mechanism of this part of the system:

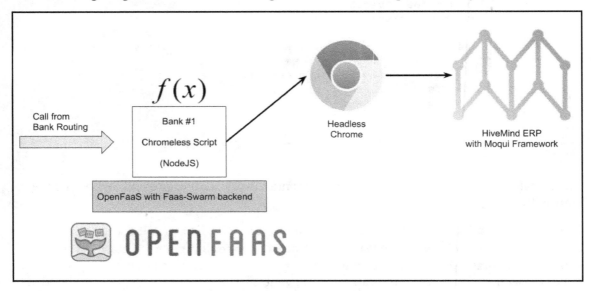

Figure 8.11: Diagram of implementing an OpenFaaS function to wrap around a UI-based ERP

What does `chromeless` do? `chromeless` is a Node.js library that can be used to perform browser automation, similar to PhantomJS or Selenium. But it is really fast. Together with headless Chrome instances, `chromeless` yields a very fast performance. So it could be used as a serverless function.

We start by using FaaS CLI to create a project. We call this function `hivectl`, a program to control an ERP program built with the Moqui framework, HiveMind. We will talk about HiveMind shortly after setting up this function:

```
$ faas new hivectl --lang node
2018/03/04 22:28:49 No templates found in current directory.
2018/03/04 22:28:50 Attempting to expand templates from
https://github.com/openfaas/templates.git
2018/03/04 22:28:55 Fetched 11 template(s) : [csharp dockerfile go go-armhf
node node-arm64 node-armhf python python-armhf python3 ruby] from
https://github.com/openfaas/templates.git
Folder: hivectl created.

$ cd hivectl
```

Here's the content of `hivectl.yml`, the OpenFaaS function descriptor for the `hivectl` function:

```
provider:
  name: faas
  gateway: http://localhost:8080

functions:
  hivectl:
    lang: node
    handler: ./hivectl
    image: chanwit/hivectl:0.4
```

Here's a sample configuration to make `chromeless` connect to headless Chrome running inside another container on the same network. The trick is to set `launchChrome` to `false`, and set `cdp`, **Chrome DevTool Protocol**, pointing to `host: 'chrome'`, `port: 9222`:

```
const chromeless = new Chromeless({
  launchChrome: false,
  cdp: { host: 'chrome', port: 9222, secure: false, closeTab: true }
})
```

Here is the main `chromeless` script to remotely control a headless Chrome instance. We will put the program into `hivectl/handler.js`:

```
const { Chromeless } = require('chromeless')
const url =
'http://hivemind/vapps/hmadmin/Accounting/FinancialAccount/FinancialAccount
Trans?finAccountId='

module.exports = (content, callback) => {

  async function run(accountId, amount) {

    const chromeless = new Chromeless({
      launchChrome: false,
      cdp: { host: 'chrome', port: 9222, secure: false, closeTab: true }
    })

    const screenshot = await chromeless
      .goto('http://hivemind/Login/logout')
      .click('#TestLoginLink_button')
      .wait('.btn-danger')
      .goto(url + accountId)
      .wait('#AdjustDialog-button')
      .click('#AdjustDialog-button')
      .type(amount, '#AdjustFinancialAccount_amount')
```

```
        .mousedown('#select2-AdjustFinancialAccount_reasonEnumId-container')
        .mouseup('#select2-AdjustFinancialAccount_reasonEnumId-container')
        .press(40, 5)
        .press(13)
        .click('#AdjustFinancialAccount_submitButton')
        .screenshot()
        .catch(e => {
          console.log('{"error":"' + e.message + '"}')
          process.exit(1);
        })

    console.log('{"success": "ok", "screenshot":"' + screenshot + '"}')

    await chromeless.end()
  }

  const opt = JSON.parse(content)
  run(opt.accountId, opt.amount).catch(console.error.bind(console))

};
```

With OpenFaaS, we can simply build the function container with the following command:

```
$ faas build -f ./hivectl.yml
...
Successfully built 1f7cc398fc61
Successfully tagged chanwit/hivectl:0.4
Image: chanwit/hivectl:0.4 built.
[0] < Building hivectl done.
[0] worker done.
```

Next, we will define the function in OpenFaaS. On the OpenFaaS UI, define a new function and the dialog will allow us to attach the new function to a specific network, `parse_net` in this case:

- **Image:** `chanwit/hivectl:0.4`
- **Name:** `hivectl`
- **Network:** `parse_net`

We start a headless Chrome instance, exposing it as `chrome` on the same network as the caller function. This Chrome headless will be listening on TCP port `9222`:

```
docker run -d --network=parse_net \
    --network-alias=chrome \
    --cap-add=SYS_ADMIN \
    justinribeiro/chrome-headless
```

We now start an ERP system. It is the HiveMind ERP built using the Moqui framework. We can download it from the Moqui repository on GitHub (`https://github.com/moqui/moqui-framework`). Fortunately, the Moqui team also prepares a Docker image for use. So just run it and attach it to the main `parse_net`. Port `10000` is published only for debugging purposes:

```
$ docker run -p 10000:80 \
    -d --network=parse_net \
    --network-alias=hivemind \
    moqui/hivemind
```

The following screenshot shows the financial account page that will be processed by the `chromeless` function:

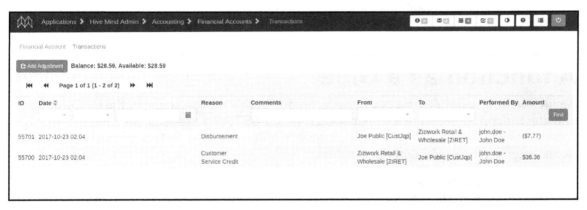

Figure 8.12: The HiveMind financial account page

Going back to the **back routing,** here's the code inside the WebHook (running on Fn) calling to the `hivectl` function (running on OpenFaaS). The WebHook code creates an HTTP client, then sends two parameters, `accountId` and `amount`, to the `hivectl` function:

```
public boolean faasAdjust(String txId,
                          String accountId,
                          Double amount) throws Exception {
    val env = System.getenv("FAAS_GATEWAY_SERVICE");
    val faasGatewayService = (env == null? "http://gateway:8080" : env);

    val JSON = MediaType.parse("application/json; charset=utf-8");
    val client = new OkHttpClient();
    val json = new ObjectMapper().writeValueAsString(new
HashMap<String,String>(){{
        put("accountId", accountId);
        put("amount", String.valueOf(amount));
```

```
    }});
    val body = RequestBody.create(JSON, json);
    val request = new Request.Builder()
            .url(faasGatewayService + "/function/hivectl")
            .post(body)
            .build();
    val response = client.newCall(request).execute();
    System.out.println(response);

    if(response.code() == 200) {
        val str = response.body().string();
        return true;
    }

      throw new Exception(response.toString());
}
```

A function as a Glue

Besides writing a simple processor, the technique in this section is one of the simplest forms of using functions. We have a bank backend with REST APIs exposed. So we write a function as a Glue to hide the complex interface of the backend. In this example, we use Go as the language to implement the function.

The scenario is that we have a REST API server and we want to unify it with another similar service. In the example in this chapter, we have two banking backends with different ways of interaction. The first one is a web-based UI without a REST interface, another one is the REST API in this section:

```
func main() {
  input := os.Args[1]

  // OpenWhisk params are key/value paris
  params := map[string]interface{}{}
  err := json.Unmarshal([]byte(input), params)
  if err != nil {
    fmt.Printf(`{"error":"%s", "input": "%s"}`, err.Error(), string(input))
    os.Exit(-1)
  }

  entry := Entry{
    Account: Account{
      Id: params["accountId"].(string),
    },
```

```
        Amount: params["amount"].(float64),
    }

    jsonValue, err := json.Marshal(entry)
    if err != nil {
        fmt.Printf(`{"error":"%s"}`, err.Error())
        os.Exit(-1)
    }

    accountService := os.Getenv("ACCOUNT_SERVICE")
    if accountService == "" {
        accountService = "http://accounting:8080/entries"
    }

    resp, err := http.Post(accountService,
        "application/json",
        bytes.NewBuffer(jsonValue))

    if err != nil {
        fmt.Printf(`{"error":"%s"}`, err.Error())
        os.Exit(-1)
    }

    if resp.StatusCode >= 200 resp.StatusCode <= 299 {
        fmt.Println(`{"success": "ok"}`)
        os.Exit(0)
    }

    fmt.Printf(`{"error": "%s"}`, resp.Status)
}
```

We use the multi-stage build. The `go build` command used here in the first stage is to produce static binary. Then we copy it to the second stage, `/action/exec`:

```
# Stage 0
FROM golang:1.8.5-alpine3.6

WORKDIR /go/src/app
COPY account_ctl.go .

RUN CGO_ENABLED=0 GOOS=linux GOARCH=amd64 go build -a -tags netgo -ldflags
'-extldflags "-static"' -o exec account_ctl.go

# Stage 1
FROM openwhisk/dockerskeleton

ENV FLASK_PROXY_PORT 8080
```

```
COPY --from=0 /go/src/app/exec /action/
RUN chmod +x /action/exec

CMD ["/bin/bash", "-c", "cd actionProxy python -u actionproxy.py"]
```

 Do not forget to push the image onto Docker Hub before proceeding to the next step.

Then we define the function using `wsk` CLI commands:

```
$ docker build -t chanwit/account_ctl:v1 .
$ docker push chanwit/account_ctl:v1

$ wsk -i action delete account_ctl
$ wsk -i action create --docker=chanwit/account_ctl:v1 account_ctl
```

To make a container able to talk to other FaaS platform gateways, we need to change the OpenWhisk invoker's configuration to start every container inside the `parse_net` network. The invoker image is fixed to `3a7dce` and the OpenWhisk network configuration in the environment variable section of the invoker service, `CONFIG_whisk_containerFactory_containerArgs_network`, is set to `parse_net`:

```
invoker:
    image:
openwhisk/invoker@sha256:3a7dcee078905b47306f3f06c78eee53372a4a9bf47cdd8eaf
e0194745a9b8d6
    command: /bin/sh -c "exec /init.sh 0 >> /logs/invoker-local_logs.log 2>
1"
    privileged: true
    pid: "host"
    userns_mode: "host"
    links:
      - db:db.docker
      - kafka:kafka.docker
      - zookeeper:zookeeper.docker
    depends_on:
      - db
      - kafka
    env_file:
      - ./docker-whisk-controller.env # env vars shared
      - ~/tmp/openwhisk/local.env # generated during make setup
    environment:
      COMPONENT_NAME: invoker
```

```
SERVICE_NAME: invoker0
PORT: 8085

KAFKA_HOSTS: kafka.docker:9092
ZOOKEEPER_HOSTS: zookeeper.docker:2181

DB_PROVIDER: CouchDB
DB_PROTOCOL: http
DB_PORT: 5984
DB_HOST: db.docker
DB_USERNAME: whisk_admin
DB_PASSWORD: some_passw0rd

EDGE_HOST: ${DOCKER_COMPOSE_HOST}
EDGE_HOST_APIPORT: 443

CONFIG_whisk_containerFactory_containerArgs_network: parse_net

WHISK_API_HOST_NAME: ${DOCKER_COMPOSE_HOST}
volumes:
  - ~/tmp/openwhisk/invoker/logs:/logs
  - /var/run/docker.sock:/var/run/docker.sock
  - /var/lib/docker/containers:/containers
  - /sys/fs/cgroup:/sys/fs/cgroup
ports:
  - "8085:8085"
```

To unify them, we create a function to wrap around the REST API and make both of the interfaces as similar as possible.

To start the REST API server, we use the docker run command and attach it to the parse_net with the accounting alias. Port 18080 is published for debugging purposes only:

```
docker run -p 18080:8080 -d \
  --network=parse_net \
  --network-alias=accounting \
  --name accounting \
  chanwit/accounting:0.1
```

A stream processor

Another use case of a function is to use it as a processor for data streams. A stream may be sent out from any kind of sources, such as data buses or event buses. Kafka, Twitter, or blockchain (in our case, Ethereum) could be a source of data streams. An Ethereum blockchain could emit events specific to some smart contracts when a certain action is taken.

To observe these events in the form of data streams efficiently, we need to use a kind of reactive client. RxJava is one of them. Fortunately, `web3j`, the Ethereum client we are using, already has RxJava observables to receive streaming data from an Ethereum blockchain.

We call this component `listener`. The following diagram shows what we will implement around the **Event Listener**:

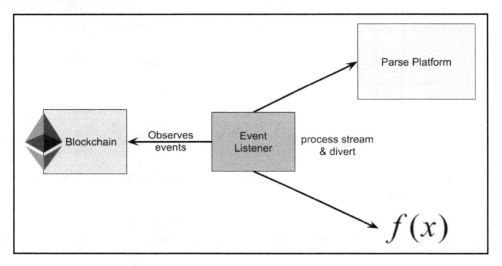

Figure 8.13: Diagram illustrating relations around the Event Listener

A requirement is that we run the agent (**Event Listener**) as a container on the same network as the blockchain. We use the agent to divert each transaction information to other endpoints. In this example, we have two endpoints. The first one is the record inside Parse. Another one is the S3-compatible storage, Minio. We upload a file to Minio when the transaction is completed.

The following shows how to use a contract observable to listen to blockchain events:

```
public class Main {

    public static void main(String[] args) throws Exception {

        val tsrContract = ContractRegistry.unlock((web3j, tm) -> {
            return TransferStateRepository.load(
                    "0x62d69f6867a0a084c6d313943dc22023bc263691",
                    web3j, tm, ManagedTransaction.GAS_PRICE,
Contract.GAS_LIMIT);
        });

        tsrContract.transferCompletedEventObservable(
            DefaultBlockParameterName.LATEST,
            DefaultBlockParameterName.LATEST).subscribe(event -> {

            System.out.printf("Transfer completed: %s\n", event.txId );

        });
    }


}
```

We use a simple Gradle build script for this component. The project can be built using the `gradle installDist` command as usual:

```
plugins {
    id 'io.franzbecker.gradle-lombok' version '1.11'
    id 'java'
    id 'application'
}

mainClassName = "event.listener.Main"

repositories {
    mavenCentral()
    jcenter()
}

dependencies {
    compile 'org.slf4j:slf4j-api:1.7.21'
    compile 'org.web3j:core:3.2.0'

    testCompile 'junit:junit:4.12'
}
```

Here's the Dockerfile for this component:

```
FROM openjdk:8u151-jdk-alpine

RUN mkdir /app
COPY ./build/install/listener/lib/*.jar /app/

ENV BLOCKCHAIN_SERVICE http://blockchain:8545/

WORKDIR /app
CMD ["java", "-cp", "*", "event.listener.Main"]
```

This is the Gradle build step, `docker build` and `docker push` command:

```
$ gradle installDist

$ docker build -t chanwit/listener:v1 .
$ docker push chanwit/listener:v1
```

Inter-FaaS platform networking

To make all functions of different platforms able to talk together, we need to set up a proper container network. The demo project discussed in this chapter is not a simple FaaS example. It is a complex scenario where functions are allowed to call other functions on the different FaaS platforms.

Normally, on some serverless platforms such as Lambda, we may sometimes assume that all functions run on the flat network of the provider. In contrast, when we run functions on our own platforms, we could segment the networks ourselves and function networking will become a challenge. However, networking will be relatively simple because the networking model in Docker and Swarm is the flat network.

How can we achieve this? By the following:

1. We create an attachable Swarm-scoped network
2. We start a FaaS framework and make its gateway attach to that network
3. We also need to tell the framework that it must attach that network to every container it created

In OpenFaas, it allows you to create a function to run on a specific network. In OpenWhisk, we can specify this with a configuration of an invoker. For the Fn Project, we need an additional hack. Here's the change required to patch to Fn in order to make it able to attach function containers to a specified network (FN_NETWORK):

```
var networkingConfig *docker.NetworkingConfig
fnNetwork := os.Getenv("FN_NETWORK")
if fnNetwork != "" {
    log.Debugf("Env FN_NETWORK found: %s. Create container %s with
network.",
                fnNetwork, task.Id())
    networkingConfig = docker.NetworkingConfig{
        EndpointsConfig: map[string]*docker.EndpointConfig{
            fnNetwork: {
                Aliases: []string{task.Id()},
            },
        },
    }
}
container := docker.CreateContainerOptions{
    Name: task.Id(),
    Config: docker.Config{
        Env: envvars,
        Cmd: cmd,
        Memory: int64(task.Memory()),
        MemorySwap: int64(task.Memory()),
        KernelMemory: int64(task.Memory()),
        CPUShares: drv.conf.CPUShares,
        Hostname: drv.hostname,
        Image: task.Image(),
        Volumes: map[string]struct{}{},
        OpenStdin: true,
        AttachStdin: true,
        StdinOnce: true,
    },
    HostConfig: docker.HostConfig{
        LogConfig: docker.LogConfig{
            Type: "none",
        },
    },
    NetworkingConfig: networkingConfig,
    Context: ctx,
}
```

The version with the function networking patch is available at https://github.com/chanwit/fn.

Exercises

This chapter covers a lot of practices and hacks to make the whole stack of the demo project, a mobile payment system, work. Please go through the content of all the sections in this chapter:

1. Why do we need to hack the Fn to build a custom version of an Fn server?
2. What is the concept of inter-FaaS platform networking? Why is it important?
3. What are the two roles of an Ethereum block in the demo project?
4. What is the data type of the parameters of an OpenWhisk function?
5. How can we encode JSON in Java with Fn?
6. How can we encode JSON in Golang?
7. What is the Parse platform?
8. What is the role of Parse WebHook?
9. What is the concept of a Glue function?
10. How can we write a function to wrap a legacy web-based application?

Summary

This chapter demonstrated a use case by showing how we can develop a mobile payment system on FaaS platforms.

We used Parse as a UI backend. Then we connected Parse to a bank routing function running on Fn via the Parse WebHook mechanism. We then demonstrated that with functions, it was relatively easy to make a call to a modern infrastructure such as blockchain. We simulated two banks to show use cases of a function, a function as a Glue, and a function that wrapped legacy systems. Then we demonstrated how a function was used in conjunction with a streaming agent to process data streams.

All of the three FaaS platforms were linked together and run on the same Docker Swarm cluster. It was quite simple to link OpenWhisk and OpenFaaS functions together, but in the case of Fn, it was a bit of a hack because the current version of Fn doesn't allow you to define a container network.

The next chapter will be the final chapter of this book. We will conclude the concept of a function and look forward to see what's next beyond the world of FaaS.

The Future of Serverless 9

This chapter discusses what lies ahead beyond FaaS. We will start by discussing a new experimental technique to restore the speed of the container runtime by introducing RunF, a libcontainer-based runtime designed for invoking immutable function containers. This chapter will continue the discussion of the possibility of using LinuxKit to prepare immutable infrastructure for FaaS platforms in general. We conclude this chapter by exploring a new architecture to hybrid the FaaS architecture on-premises with the serverless architecture on the public cloud.

Before going to these topics, let's start by summarizing what we have learned so far.

The following topics will be covered in this chapter:

- FaaS and Docker reviews
- Runtime for function containers
- LinuxKit – immutable infrastructure for FaaS
- Beyond serverless
- Declarative containers

FaaS and Docker reviews

In this book, we introduced serverless, the FaaS platforms, and how Docker is relevant to this technology. We learned together about how to set up Docker Swarm clusters on production.

The book discussed three well-known FaaS platforms, which are *OpenFaaS*, *OpenWhisk*, and the *Fn Project*. OpenFaaS uses the Swarm-based orchestrator, while OpenWhisk and Fn used their own scheduling techniques on plain Docker.

Then, we demonstrated a project in `Chapter 8`, *Putting Them All Together*, to present how we can link all of these three platforms together, by running them on the same network of a Docker cluster. The project was demonstrated on how we could invoke the services of other FaaS platforms. Functions written in several programming languages were presented including Java, Go, and JavaScript (Node.js).

We used Java to write a simple function. For modern programming models, we could use the RxJava library to help writing Java programs in the reactive style, which fit very nicely for the event-driven programming.

With JavaScript, we wrote a Chrome-based scripting to connect through. We also deployed a blockchain to demonstrate that it works nicely with the FaaS computing model.

In the following sections, we will discuss some advanced, experimental topics that go deeply or beyond the current scope of serverless and FaaS. However, some of them may be going to be mainstream in the near future.

Runtime for function containers

One of the most important components of the container ecosystem is the **container runtime**. During the early days of Docker, the runtime was LXC, then it changed to be the Docker-owned libcontainer. The libcontainer was later donated to **OCI**, the **Open Container Initiative** project under the Linux Foundation. Later, Project RunC was started. RunC is a command-line wrapper around libcontainer to enable developers to start containers from a Terminal. A developer could start a container by invoking the RunC binary and passing a root filesystem and a container specification to it.

RunC is an extremely stable piece of software. It has been with Docker since version 1.12 and is already used by millions of users. The `docker run` command actually sends its parameters to another daemon, containerd, which converts that information into a configuration file for RunC.

RunC makes the dependencies simpler as we need only a single binary, a root filesystem, and a configuration file to start a container.

As RunC is a thin wrapper around libcontainer, its code is straightforward. It is relatively easy to directly make use of libcontainer with some Go programming knowledge. The only drawback of RunC is that it is designed and built to run containers in general. In the next section, we will introduce *RunF*, a minimal runtime designed specially for running function containers efficiently.

Meet RunF

This section introduces RunF. It is a RunC counterpart that is designed for running immutable function containers. RunF is an experimental project that uses *libcontainer* to implement a new runtime to run containers in the read-only and rootless environment. Containers started with RunF are expected to be running efficiently, even inside other containers. RunF allows rootless container execution by mapping a non-root user from the host to the root user's ID inside the container.

How can we use it? The following diagram illustrates the scenario. We have a FaaS platform, and the **Gateway** accepts the incoming request and forwards it to the function **Initiator**. Through the **Event Bus**, a **Function Executor** then uses it rather than Docker to invoke the function container. With this architecture, we can improve the overall performance of the platform:

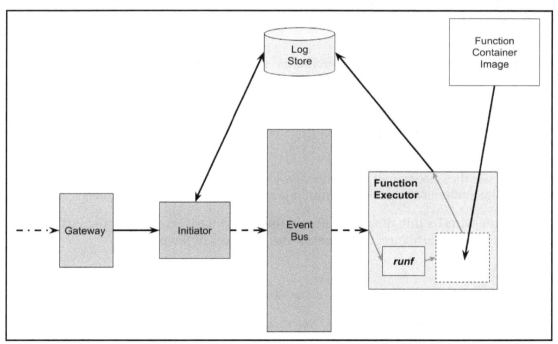

Figure 9.1: The block diagram illustrating a FaaS architecture with RunF as its runtime

A rootless container is a container allowed to run without the root user, such as in AWS Lambda. We want an immutable version of a function with read-only and rootless, because rootless containers make the system and infrastructure more secure.

Then there is a network constraint. A function should not be aware of any network-related configuration. All current FaaS platforms we have implemented so far have this limitation. Say we need to attach a running function to a certain network in order to make it work correctly, and be able to resolve names of other dependent services.

We found during Chapter 8, *Putting Them All Together*, that it is tricky to make a function container work virtually with any network provided by the platform. *RunF* is designed to solve this issue by letting the function container use the outer container network namespace. With this execution model, the *function proxy* is responsible for attaching itself to the networks, and the function container will also use these networks to access other services. If the function container runs inside the container of the function proxy, all network configuration could be eliminated.

Performance-wise with a special container runtime such as *RunF*, it is possible to cache all necessary filesystems inside each function proxy, and make them immutable. With this, we can achieve the highest possible performance similar to the way the mechanism of hot functions work.

Now let's see what's inside the implementation to make it meet all requirements:

- Immutable
- Rootless
- Host networking by default
- Zero configuration.

We mostly use the libcontainer APIs directly. Here, we explain the details to show how RunF uses libcontainer to achieve the mutable runtime for function containers.

The program starts by initializing the libcontainer, with the `Cgroupfs` configuration, to say that libcontainer will use `Cgroup` to control the resources of the process:

```
func main() {

  containerId := namesgenerator.GetRandomName(0)

  factory, err := libcontainer.New("/tmp/runf",
    libcontainer.Cgroupfs,
    libcontainer.InitArgs(os.Args[0], "init"))
  if err != nil {
    logrus.Fatal(err)
    return
  }
```

The following snippet creates a config. The default location of the rootfs is ./rootfs under the current directory. We set the flag Readonlyfs to be true for the immutable filesystem. NoNewPrivileges is set to true so as to not allow the process to gain any new privilege. Rootless being true is designed to tell us that we will map non-root UID and GID to the container's root ID. After the initial flags, we then set the capability of the process. Here's the list:

- CAP_AUDIT_WRITE is the ability to write to the kernel's audit logs
- CAP_KILL is the ability for the process to send the signals
- CAP_NET_BIND_SERVICE is the ability to bind a socket to the privileged ports

```
defaultMountFlags := unix.MS_NOEXEC | unix.MS_NOSUID | unix.MS_NODEV

cwd, err := os.Getwd()
currentUser, err := user.Current()
uid, err := strconv.Atoi(currentUser.Uid)
gid, err := strconv.Atoi(currentUser.Gid)
caps := []string{
  "CAP_AUDIT_WRITE",
  "CAP_KILL",
  "CAP_NET_BIND_SERVICE",
}

config := &configs.Config{
  Rootfs:          cwd + "/rootfs",
  Readonlyfs:      true,
  NoNewPrivileges: true,
  Rootless:        true,
  Capabilities: &configs.Capabilities{
    Bounding:    caps,
    Permitted:   caps,
    Inheritable: caps,
    Ambient:     caps,
    Effective:   caps,
  },
```

The Namespaces property is one of the most important settings of the container runtime. Within this block of configuration, we set it to use the following namespaces, NS, UTS (hostname and domain name), IPC, PID, and USER. The user namespace, NSUSER, is the key setting to allow running containers in the rootless mode. We left out the NET namespace. The reason is that runf will start a function container inside another container, the *function executor*. Without the NET namespace isolation, the function container will use the same network namespace as the outside container, so it will be able to access any service attached to the network of the function executor.

Another setting is the `Cgroup` setting. This setting allows hierarchical control resources of the process. This is mostly the default configuration:

```
Namespaces: configs.Namespaces([]configs.Namespace{
  {Type: configs.NEWNS},
  {Type: configs.NEWUTS},
  {Type: configs.NEWIPC},
  {Type: configs.NEWPID},
  {Type: configs.NEWUSER},
}),
Cgroups: &configs.Cgroup{
  Name:      "runf",
  Parent:    "system",
  Resources: &configs.Resources{
    MemorySwappiness: nil,
    AllowAllDevices:  nil,
    AllowedDevices:   configs.DefaultAllowedDevices,
  },
},
```

`MaskPaths` and `ReadonlyPaths` are set as the following. This setting is mainly to prevent the changes made by the running process to the system:

```
MaskPaths: []string{
  "/proc/kcore",
  "/proc/latency_stats",
  "/proc/timer_list",
  "/proc/timer_stats",
  "/proc/sched_debug",
  "/sys/firmware",
  "/proc/scsi",
},
ReadonlyPaths: []string{
  "/proc/asound",
  "/proc/bus",
  "/proc/fs",
  "/proc/irq",
  "/proc/sys",
  "/proc/sysrq-trigger",
},
```

All devices are set to be auto created. Then, the Mount setting defines a set of filesystems required to mount from the host into the container. In the case of RunF, it is a nested mounted from the function executor to the function container:

```
Devices: configs.DefaultAutoCreatedDevices,
Hostname: containerId,
Mounts: []*configs.Mount{
   {
      Source:        "proc",
      Destination:   "/proc",
      Device:        "proc",
      Flags:         defaultMountFlags,
   },
   {
      Source:        "tmpfs",
      Destination:   "/dev",
      Device:        "tmpfs",
      Flags:         unix.MS_NOSUID | unix.MS_STRICTATIME,
      Data:          "mode=755",
   },
   {
      Device:        "devpts",
      Source:        "devpts",
      Destination:   "/dev/pts",
      Flags:         unix.MS_NOSUID | unix.MS_NOEXEC,
      Data:          "newinstance,ptmxmode=0666,mode=0620",
   },
   {
      Device:        "tmpfs",
      Source:        "shm",
      Destination:   "/dev/shm",
      Flags:         defaultMountFlags,
      Data:          "mode=1777,size=65536k",
   },
},
```

Here's the UID and GID mapping from the host ID (HostID) to the ID inside the container (ContainerID). In the following example, we map the current user ID to the ID of the root user inside the container:

```
Rlimits: []configs.Rlimit{
   {
      Type: unix.RLIMIT_NOFILE,
      Hard: uint64(1024),
      Soft: uint64(1024),
   },
},
```

```
      UidMappings: []configs.IDMap{
         {
            ContainerID: 0,
            HostID:      uid,
            Size:        1,
         },
      },
      GidMappings: []configs.IDMap{
         {
            ContainerID: 0,
            HostID:      gid,
            Size:        1,
         },
      },
   }
```

We use libcontainer's factor to create a container with the generated ID and the `config` we have set:

```
container, err := factory.Create(containerId, config)
if err != nil {
  logrus.Fatal(err)
  return
}
```

Then, we prepare environment variables. They are simply an *array of strings*. Each element is a *key=value* pair of each variable that we'd like to set for the process. We prepare a process to run using `libcontainer.Process`. Process input, output, and error are redirected to the default standard counterparts:

```
environmentVars := []string{
   "PATH=/usr/local/sbin:/usr/local/bin:/usr/sbin:/usr/bin:/sbin:/bin",
   "HOSTNAME=" + containerId,
   "TERM=xterm",
}
process := &libcontainer.Process{
   Args:    os.Args[1:],
   Env:     environmentVars,
   User:    "root",
   Cwd:     "/",
   Stdin:   os.Stdin,
   Stdout:  os.Stdout,
   Stderr:  os.Stderr,
}

err = container.Run(process)
if err != nil {
```

```
    container.Destroy()
    logrus.Fatal(err)
    return
  }

  _, err = process.Wait()
  if err != nil {
    logrus.Fatal(err)
  }

  defer container.Destroy()
}
```

We will then prepare and build the runf binary. This requires *libcontainer* and other few to build. We normally use the go get command to do so. After that, just simply build with the go build command:

```
$ go get golang.org/x/sys/unix
$ go get github.com/Sirupsen/logrus
$ go get github.com/docker/docker/pkg/namesgenerator
$ go get github.com/opencontainers/runc/libcontainer

$ go build runf.go
```

To prepare a root filesystem, we use undocker.py together with the docker save command. The undocker.py script can be downloaded from https://github.com/larsks/undocker.

Here's the command to prepare a root filesystem to the rootfs directory from the busybox image:

```
$ docker save busybox | ./undocker.py --output rootfs -W -i busybox
```

Now, let's test running some containers. We will see that the ls command lists files inside a container:

```
$ ./runf ls
bin dev etc home proc root sys tmp usr var
```

Within a Docker network

Next, we will try something a bit advanced by preparing a small system that looks similar to the following diagram. The scenario is that we would like a container started by **runf** inside another container, **wrapper-runf** (which is, in reality, a function executor), to connect to some network services running on the same Docker network, **test_net**:

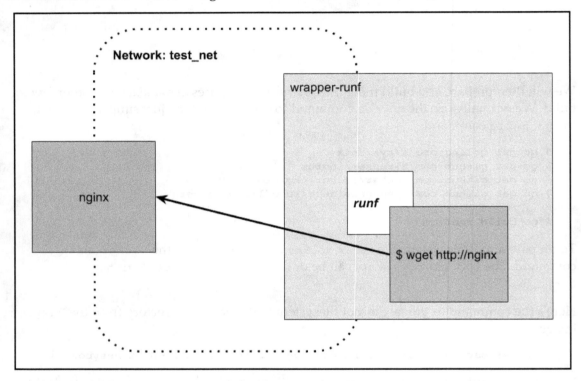

Figure 9.2: An example of using RunF inside a Docker network

The trick is that we put `resolv.conf` from the standard Docker Swarm mode as `./rootfs/etc/resolv.conf` to make the process inside the nested container be able to resolve all service names on the attached Docker network. Here's the content of `resolv.conf`:

```
search domain.name
nameserver 127.0.0.11
options ndots:0
```

Then we prepare a Dockerfile for the `wrapper-runf` container:

```
FROM ubuntu:latest

RUN apt-get update && apt-get install -y curl

WORKDIR /root

COPY ./runf /usr/bin/runf
COPY rootfs /root/rootfs
COPY resolv.conf /root/rootfs/etc/resolv.conf
```

We can build it normally with the `docker build` command:

```
$ docker build -t wrapper-runf .
```

The following snippet is the preparation for creating a Docker network, attaching `nginx` to the network, then running a `wrapper-runf` container with `/bin/bash` there.

Finally, we start a nested container with `runf` that connects to `nginx`:

```
$ docker network create -d overlay --attachable test_net

$ docker run -d \
  --network=test_net \
  --network-alias=nginx \
  nginx

$ docker run --rm -it \
  --network=test_net \
  --privileged \
  -v /sys/fs/cgroup:/sys/fs/cgroup \
  wrapper-runf /bin/bash

/ # runf wget http://nginx
```

What's next?

With `runf`, it is potentially a way to move towards another step of fast and immutable functions with a special runtime. What you can try is to implement a proxy container wrapping around `runf` and make it run functions inside the real platform. This is left as an (a bit advanced) exercise.

LinuxKit – immutable infrastructure for FaaS

LinuxKit is a set of tools for preparing immutable sets of infrastructure. It is designed to compose containers into a ready-to-use OS. Of course, an OS produced by LinuxKit is for running containers. To make an immutable and scalable infrastructure for FaaS platforms, LinuxKit is one of the best choices out there.

Here's a sample of a LinuxKit YAML file to build an immutable OS for Docker. The kernel block is saying that this OS will boot with Linux Kernel 4.14.23. The `boot` command, `cmdline`, says that the kernel will be starting with consoles on four different TTYs:

```
kernel:
  image: linuxkit/kernel:4.14.23
  cmdline: "console=tty0 console=ttyS0 console=ttyAMA0 console=ttysclp0"
```

The four next containers declared inside the `init` block are the base programs that will be unpacked directly onto the filesystem. All the `init` level programs include `runc` and `containerd`. Also, the CA certificates will be installed directly onto the filesystem before the programs declared in the next, `onboot`, block can proceed:

```
init:
  - linuxkit/init:b212cfeb4bb6330e0a7547d8010fe2e8489b677a
  - linuxkit/runc:7c39a68490a12cde830e1922f171c451fb08e731
  - linuxkit/containerd:37e397ebfc6bd5d8e18695b121166ffd0cbfd9f0
  - linuxkit/ca-certificates:v0.2
```

The `onboot` block and the `mountie` command will automatically mount the first available partition to `/var/lib/docker`. Please note that LinuxKit only allows you to mount to the directory under the `/var` directory:

```
onboot:
  - name: sysctl
    image: linuxkit/sysctl:v0.2
  - name: sysfs
    image: linuxkit/sysfs:v0.2
  - name: format
    image: linuxkit/format:v0.2
  - name: mount
    image: linuxkit/mount:v0.2
    command: ["/usr/bin/mountie", "/var/lib/docker"]
```

The services block declares system containers, which serve as long running services. All these services are run and maintained by containers, started by the init process in the init block.

A service declared in this block can be started in any order.

In the following example, docker is one of the services. Docker image, docker:17.09.0-ce-dind, is used for running this Docker service. This service runs on the host network. This is basically the same concept as RancherOS. This instance of dockerd run by the docker service is the user-level container management system, while containerd from the init block is the system-level container management system. Other system containers here are rngd—a random number generator daemon, dhcpd—an DHCP service, and ntpd—the OpenNTPD daemon for syncing the machine clock, for example:

```
services:
  - name: getty
    image: linuxkit/getty:v0.2
    env:
     - INSECURE=true
  - name: rngd
    image: linuxkit/rngd:v0.2
  - name: dhcpcd
    image: linuxkit/dhcpcd:v0.2
  - name: ntpd
    image: linuxkit/openntpd:v0.2
  - name: docker
    image: docker:17.09.0-ce-dind
    capabilities:
     - all
    net: host
    mounts:
     - type: cgroup
       options: ["rw","nosuid","noexec","nodev","relatime"]
    binds:
     - /etc/resolv.conf:/etc/resolv.conf
     - /var/lib/docker:/var/lib/docker
     - /lib/modules:/lib/modules
     - /etc/docker/daemon.json:/etc/docker/daemon.json
    command: ["/usr/local/bin/docker-init", "/usr/local/bin/dockerd"]
```

The file block is for declaring *files* or *directories* that we would like to have on our immutable filesystem. In the following example, we declare `/var/lib/docker` and create a Docker's daemon configuration `/etc/docker/daemon.json` with the content `{"debug": true}` inside it. These files are created during the image's build phase:

```
files:
  - path: var/lib/docker
    directory: true
  - path: etc/docker/daemon.json
    contents: '{"debug": true}'
trust:
  org:
    - linuxkit
    - library
```

We have another example of the `files` block. This is the standard way to put our public key into the filesystem image. The attribute `mode` is for setting the file mode when copying the file to the final image. In this example, we require the public key file to be `0600`. With this configuration and the running `sshd` service, we will be allowed to remotely SSH into the machine:

```
files:
  - path: root/.ssh/authorized_keys
    source: ~/.ssh/id_rsa.pub
    mode: "0600"
    optional: true
```

Here's the step to build the LinuxKit command line:

```
$ go get -u github.com/linuxkit/linuxkit/src/cmd/linuxkit
```

If we have already installed the Go programming language using GVM, the binary will be available to run.

We'll build a Docker OS, available at `https://github.com/linuxkit/linuxkit/blob/master/examples/docker.yml`:

```
$ linuxkit build docker.yml
Extract kernel image: linuxkit/kernel:4.14.26
Pull image: docker.io/linuxkit/kernel:4.14.26@sha256:9368a ...
...
Add files:
  var/lib/docker
  etc/docker/daemon.json
Create outputs:
  docker-kernel docker-initrd.img docker-cmdline
```

Beyond serverless

Hybrid serverless would be a deployment model that links hybrid cloud to the serverless deployment model. It is already started by IT vendors offering hardware rental services in the form of private clouds, putting them to customer's organizations, and charging at the rate of pay-as-you-go.

When the serverless and FaaS computing platforms are deployed on top of that kind of hybrid infrastructure, they become **hybrid serverless**. This could be the next generation of computing platform that allows you to store sensitive data inside the organization, having some important FaaS functions running on the local system, while leveraging some extra computing resources as pay-per-request. It will be in the scope of the definition of serverless, if the customer's organization does not need to maintain or administer any of the hardware servers. Fortunately, when mixing this model with what we have discussed throughout this book, using Docker as our infrastructure would still be applied to this kind of infrastructure. Docker is still a good choice for balancing between maintaining infrastructure on our own and making the serverless platforms do the rest of the work for us.

In the following diagram, the overall system shows a hybrid architecture. In the case of using a FaaS platform only from inside the organization, requests would be made firstly to the on-premises infrastructure. When loads become large, instances of the function executors would be scaled out and eventually burst to a public cloud infrastructure. However, the data stores are usually placed inside the organization. So, the outside function executors must be able to access them just as if they were running on-premises:

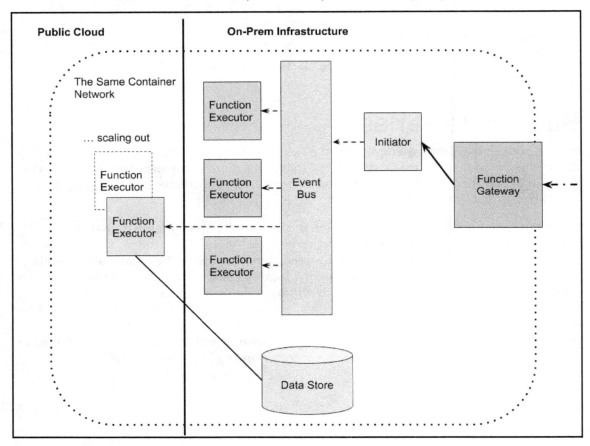

Figure 9.3: A hybrid architecture for FaaS

Declarative containers

Declarative containers could be considered as a technology in between a normal container and a container running on FaaS. Let's look at the following imaginary Dockerfile:

```
FROM openjdk:8

COPY app.jar /app/app.jar

CMD ["/opt/jdk/bin/java", "-Xmx2G", "-jar", "/app/app.jar"]
```

What do we see here? At the first time of reading, it would look like a normal Dockerfile. Yes, it is. But it's not a declarative way to define an application container. Why?

We already know that this is a Java application doing some work for us. But it has hardcoded some important and brittle configurations, for example, when openjdk:8 pinned the app to use only that implementation, while -Xmx2G limits the memory usage of the app.

All FaaS platforms these days use containers in the same way. They tie some specific configurations into function containers but actually people need a very neutral and portable way of deploying functions.

So what does a declarative container look like?

It looks something like this:

```
FROM scratch

COPY app.jar /app/app.jar

CMD ["java", "-jar", "/app/app.jar"]
```

You might think it is impossible to run this container on any runtime at the moment. The answer is you are correct. But I still argue that the application should be declared in the same way. We should remove all brittle configuration out of the Dockerfile as much as possible. Then we should let a new entity, maybe inside a container engine, manage the environment around the application for us.

For example, it is relatively easy to intercept the container creation process then compute the limitation of the memory allowed by the container (via `docker run -m` for example) and put that value into the command line of `java` to cap the memory limit at the application level. The entity responsible for this kind of work inside a container engine would be called the **Application Profile Manager**, as shown in the following diagram:

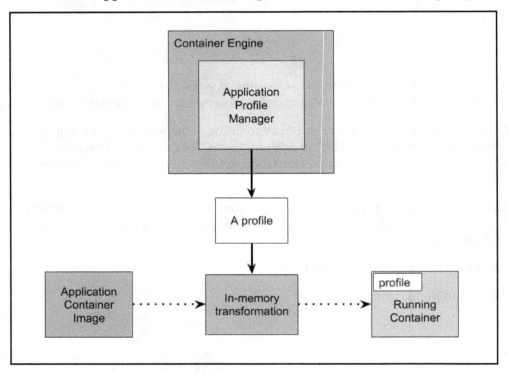

Figure 9.4: A container engine with the application profile manager

The crosscutting concept like this is nothing new. We already have a similar concept applied to Docker. Guess what? It's the security concern. Docker already has the AppArmor default profile applied to each running container with the AppArmor subsystem enabled. That's about security concerns. This is at the more application-specific level of concern, so why don't we have a similar concept to help make our life easier?

With this concept, container images would become declarative containers as there is no specific environment or configuration hardcoded for them. And it's the responsibility of the **Application Profile Manager** to selectively apply an appropriate profile for the container and make it work nicely.

What is the practical benefit of declarative containers? Here's a concrete explanation for the Java app we discussed earlier.

In the world of Java, the application architecture has been designed to decouple between the application and the runtime. With the very strong specification of the JVM, the JVM for running applications is always swappable and replaceable. For example, if we start running an application with an OpenJDK, and we are not happy with its performance, we can safely swap the JVM to be the Zulu JVM or the IBM J9.

With the declarative approach to containers, the Java runtime would be easily swappable on-the-fly without rebuilding the Docker image. It also allows you to apply JVM hot fixes to the running system.

We can download the modified version of Docker with this declarative feature for Java from `http://github.com/joconen/engine`.

Exercises

Now it's time to review all the concepts in this chapter:

1. What do you think is lying ahead after the serverless era?
2. What is the next generation of computing you might probably be thinking of?
3. What is the feature of libcontainer that allows rootless execution?
4. What are the namespaces provided by Linux?
5. Explain why RunF is able to access the network services when running inside other containers.
6. What is the benefit of using LinuxKit to prepare an infrastructure.
7. What is a declarative approach to containers? How could it apply to other application platforms, beside Java?
8. How could we design a hybrid serverless architecture when we would like to access services from outside the organization?

Summary

This chapter ends this book with a discussion of what we could use to make the FaaS moving forward. We reviewed what we have been through with Docker and three major FaaS platforms running on it.

Docker is a great infrastructure when it's considered that all these three FaaS platforms are actually using its direct feature, rather than solely relying on its orchestrator functionalities. Why? Maybe because the FaaS computing model fits this simple kind of infrastructure instead of complex ones.

What if we could simply do `docker run`, then the container is transformed into a FaaS function serving its functionality somewhere on the cluster? Function wrapper, action proxy, or function watchdog could be injected into a simple container that processes input and output via standard I/O and turns it into an online function. Then a kind of magical infrastructure will be taking care of everything for us. We are gradually moving toward to that reality.

References

1. Apache Foundation. *Apache OpenWhisk*. Available at: `https://openwhisk.apache.org/`. (Accessed: March 28, 2018).
2. Microsoft Corp. Azure functions—serverless architecture | Microsoft Azure. Available at: `https://azure.microsoft.com/en-us/services/functions/`. (Accessed: March 28, 2018).
3. Burns, B., Grant, B., Oppenheimer, D., Brewer, E. & Wilkes, J. Borg, Omega, and Kubernetes. Queue 14, 10:70–10:93 (2016).
4. Schickling, J., Lüthy, M., Suchanek, T. & et al. *chromeless: Chrome automation made simple*. (Graphcool, 2018).
5. Google Inc. Concepts | Cloud Functions. *Google Cloud* Available at: `https://cloud.google.com/functions/docs/concepts`. (Accessed: 28th March 2018).
6. Crosby, M., Day, S., Laventure, K.-M., McGowan, D. & et al. *containerd: An open and reliable container runtime*. (containerd, 2018).
7. Docker Inc. Docker. (2018). Available at: `https://www.docker.com/`. (Accessed: 28th March 2018).
8. Smith, R. *Docker Orchestration*. (Packt Publishing Ltd, 2017).
9. Merkel, D. Docker: Lightweight Linux Containers for Consistent Development and Deployment. *Linux J.* **2014**, (2014).

10. The Go Community. Documentation - The Go Programming Language. Available at: `https://golang.org/doc/`. (Accessed: 30th March 2018).

11. The Linux Foundation. Envoy Proxy - Home. Available at: `https://www.envoyproxy.io/`. (Accessed: 1st April 2018).

12. The Ethereum Foundation. Ethereum Project. Available at: `https://www.ethereum.org/`. (Accessed: 30th March 2018).

13. Avram, A. FaaS, PaaS, and the Benefits of the Serverless Architecture. *Retrieved from 'InfoQ' https://www. infoq. com/news/2016/06/faasserverless-architecture* on **28**, (2016).

14. Oracle Inc. Fn Project - The Container Native Serverless Framework. Available at: `https://fnproject.io/`. (Accessed: 28th March 2018).

15. Arimura, C., Reeder, T. & et al. *Fn: The container native, cloud agnostic serverless platform.* (Oracle inc., 2018).

16. Google Inc. Google Cloud Functions Documentation | Cloud Functions. *Google Cloud* Available at: `https://cloud.google.com/functions/docs/`. (Accessed: 28th March 2018). Kaewkasi, C. & Chuenmuneewong, K. Improvement of container scheduling for docker using ant colony optimization. in *Knowledge and Smart Technology (KST), 2017 9th International Conference on 254–259* (IEEE, 2017).

17. Apache Foundation. incubator-openwhisk: *Apache OpenWhisk is a serverless event-based programming service and an Apache Incubator project.* (The Apache Software Foundation, 2018).

18. Cormack, J. & et al. linuxkit: *A toolkit for building secure, portable and lean operating systems for containers.* (LinuxKit, 2018).

19. Janakiraman, B. Martin Fowler's bliki: Serverless. *martinfowler.com* (2016). Available at: `https://martinfowler.com/bliki/Serverless.html`. (Accessed: 28th March 2018).

20. Sharma, S. *Mastering Microservices with Java 9.* (Packt Publishing Ltd, 2017).

21. Moby Community,The. Moby. *GitHub* Available at: `https://github.com/moby`. (Accessed: 30th March 2018).

22. Moby Community,The. moby: *Moby Project* - a collaborative project for the container ecosystem to assemble container-based systems. (Moby, 2018).

23. Jones, D. E. & et al. Moqui Ecosystem. Available at: `https://www.moqui.org/`. (Accessed: 30th March 2018).

24. Soppelsa, F. & Kaewkasi, C. *Native Docker Clustering with Swarm.* (Packt Publishing - ebooks Account, 2017).

25. Marmol, V., Jnagal, R. & Hockin, T. Networking in containers and container clusters. *Proceedings of netdev 0.1, February* (2015).

26. Ellis, A. *OpenFaaS - Serverless Functions Made Simple for Docker & Kubernetes.* (OpenFaaS, 2018).

27. Amazon Web Services, Inc. Optimizing Enterprise Economics with Serverless Architectures. (2017).

28. Parse Community,The. Parse + Open Source. *Parse Open Source Hub* Available at: `http://parseplatform.org/`. (Accessed: 30th March 2018).

29. Vilmart, F. & et al. parse-server: *Parse-compatible API server module for Node/Express.* (Parse, 2018).

30. Linux Foundation,The. *runc: CLI tool for spawning and running containers according to the OCI specification.* (Open Container Initiative, 2018).

31. Christensen, B., Karnok, D. & et al. *RxJava – Reactive Extensions for the JVM – a library for composing asynchronous and event-based programs using observable sequences for the Java VM.* (ReactiveX, 2018).

32. Roberts, M. Serverless Architectures. *martinfowler.com* (2016). Available at: `https://martinfowler.com/articles/serverless.html`. (Accessed: 28th March 2018).

33. Baldini, I. et al. Serverless computing: Current trends and open problems. in *Research Advances in Cloud Computing* 1–20 (Springer, 2017).

34. GOTO Conferences. *Serverless: the Future of Software Architecture by Peter Sbarski.* (2017).

35. Fox, G. C., Ishakian, V., Muthusamy, V. & Slominski, A. Status of Serverless Computing and Function-as-a-Service (FaaS) in Industry and Research. *arXiv preprint arXiv:1708.08028* (2017).

36. Docker Inc. Swarm mode overview. *Docker Documentation (2018).* Available at: `https://docs.docker.com/engine/swarm/`. (Accessed: 28th March 2018).

37. Kaewkasi, C. & et al. *The Docker Swarm 2000 Collaborative Project.* (SwarmZilla Collaborative Project, 2016).

38. Containous. Træfik. Available at: `https://traefik.io/`. (Accessed: 1st April 2018).

39. Lubin, J. & et al. Truffle Suite - Your Ethereum Swiss Army Knife. *Truffle Suite* Available at: `http://truffleframework.com`. (Accessed: 30th March 2018).

40. Weaveworks Inc. Weave Net: Network Containers Across Environments | Weaveworks. Available at: `https://www.weave.works/oss/net/`. (Accessed:30th March 2018).

Other Books You May Enjoy

If you enjoyed this book, you may be interested in these other books by Packt:

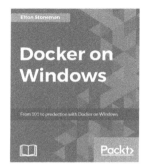

Docker on Windows
Elton Stoneman

ISBN: 978-1-78528-165-5

- Comprehend key Docker concepts: images, containers, registries, and swarms
- Run Docker on Windows 10, Windows Server 2016, and in the cloud
- Deploy and monitor distributed solutions across multiple Docker containers
- Run containers with high availability and failover with Docker Swarm
- Master security in-depth with the Docker platform, making your apps more secure
- Build a Continuous Deployment pipeline by running Jenkins in Docker
- Debug applications running in Docker containers using Visual Studio
- Plan the adoption of Docker in your own organization

Learning Docker - Second Edition
Jeeva S. Chelladhurai, Vinod Singh, Pethuru Raj

ISBN: 978-1-78646-292-3

- Develop containerized applications using the Docker version 17.03
- Build Docker images from containers and launch them
- Develop Docker images and containers leveraging Dockerfiles
- Use Docker volumes to share data
- Get to know how data is shared between containers
- Understand Docker Jenkins integration
- Gain the power of container orchestration
- Familiarize yourself with the frequently used commands such as docker exec, docker ps, docker top, and docker stats

Leave a review - let other readers know what you think

Please share your thoughts on this book with others by leaving a review on the site that you bought it from. If you purchased the book from Amazon, please leave us an honest review on this book's Amazon page. This is vital so that other potential readers can see and use your unbiased opinion to make purchasing decisions, we can understand what our customers think about our products, and our authors can see your feedback on the title that they have worked with Packt to create. It will only take a few minutes of your time, but is valuable to other potential customers, our authors, and Packt. Thank you!

Index